How To Become A United States Citizen

A Step-by-Step Guidebook for Self Instruction

Como Hacerse Ciudadano De Los Estados Unidos

Una Guia Detallada de Auto-Instruccion

by

SALLY A. ABEL

NOLO PRESS

P.O. Box 544, Occidental, CA 95465

ISBN 0-917316-60-6

Credits

Spanish Translation: Martha Oberti
Design & Production: Charles E. Sherman
Cover & Illustrations: Janet Kirwan Madison

© 1983 by Sally A. Abel

ISBN 0-917316-60-6
Library of Congress Catalog No. 83-062116

Dedication

This book is dedicated to my daddy, Johannes Wilhelmus Brand, who at age twenty, in 1923, immigrated to the United States. He came from Holland on a boat called the "New Amsterdam" in search of the American dream . . . and he found it! He lived the rest of his life as a proud American citizen, never taking America for granted. It was his example that prompted me to teach classes helping hundreds of aliens to become United States citizens and finally, to write this self-help book. May many more immigrants, like my dad, fully experience America, the land of opportunity, through United States citizenship.

Acknowledgment

We are deeply indebted to **Dan P. Danilov,** a noted immigration attorney in Seattle, Washington, for his many valuable suggestions and for his enthusiastic support throughout this project.

Mr. Danilov has practiced in the immigration law field for over 25 years. He is author of the prestigious law book, **Danilov's U.S. Immigration Law Citator,** the very popular book, **Immigrating to the U.S.A.,** and has been editor for various immigration law journals. Time taken from such a busy professional life to help with this book was an act of real generosity for which we are truly grateful.

CONTENIDO

TABLE OF CONTENTS

APÉNDICE:

LISTA DE EJEMPLARES

LIST OF SAMPLES:

Introducción

El objeto de este libro es para ayudarlo a que usted mismo pueda completar solo el procedimiento de hacerse Ciudadano de los Estados Unidos. Ya que este es un libro de auto-ayuda completo, ud. se puede preparar para la ciudadanía en la conveniencia y la comodidad de su hogar, cuando ud. tenga el tiempo disponible y a su propio compás. Ejemplares de formularios que se usan para lograrlo se le han incluido para guiarlo.

El procedimiento de naturalización, comenzando desde el momento de llenar la solicitud y terminando con la audiencia de corte final, puede tomar tan poquito como unos meses o tanto como casi dos años. Una espera de un año aproximadamente no es para nada raro. La mayoría del tiempo, la solicitud esta fuera de sus manos y se va tramitando por los oficiales federales. Asi es que es mejor comenzar inmediatamente, tan pronto como sea ud. calificado. Entre más pronto comience, más pronto se hara ud. un ciudadano.

Nota

La intención de éste libro es de proveer un informe correcto e autoritativo referente al procedimiento de la naturalización para la ciudadanía de los Estados Unidos. Todo cuidado se ha tomado para escribirlo, y los individuos necesarios y las materias de referencia apropiadas se han consultado, especialmente ésas del Servicio de Inmigración y Naturalización del Departamento de Justicia de los Estados Unidos. Sin embargo, las leyes federales tocante a la naturalización pueden ser cambiadas. Asi es que, para tener un informe detallado y al tanto, especialmente en casos complejos, el solicitante debe de consultar al Servicio de Inmigración y Naturalización de los Estados Unidos ó a un abogado de inmigración.

Introduction

The aim of this book is to help you to help yourself through the entire process of becoming a United States Citizen. Because this is a complete self-help book, you can prepare for citizenship in the convenience and comfort of home, at your leisure, and at your own pace. Samples of forms used along the way have been included to guide you.

The naturalization process, beginning with making application and ending with the final court hearing, can take as little as a few months or as long as nearly two years. A wait of about one year is not at all uncommon. Most of this time, the application is out of your hands and is being processed by federal officials. So, it is best to begin immediately, as soon as you are qualified. The sooner you start, the sooner you become a citizen.

Note

This book is intended to provide accurate and authoritative information regarding the process of naturalization for United States Citizenship. Every care has been taken in the writing of it, and appropriate individuals and reference materials have been consulted, especially those from the Immigration and Naturalization Service of the United States Department of Justice. However, federal laws regarding naturalization are subject to change. Therefore, for more detailed or updated information, particularly in complex cases, the applicant should consult the United States Immigration and Naturalization Service or an immigration attorney.

Capitulo 1
TODO REFERENTE A LA
NATURALIZACION

¿Que es la naturalización?

Sencillamente, "naturalización" quiere decir el hecho de que un extranjero se haga ciudadano. El Congreso ha pasado leyes de naturalización que exponen las condiciones para que los inmigrantes se puedan hacer ciudadanos. Tales leyes intentan que un inmigrante pueda hacerse ciudadano solamente si el, o ella, esté dispuesto a aceptar los deberes y las responsabilidades de ciudadanía y de conservar y proteger la democracia Americana. Las leyes son iguales para los hombres y las mujeres de toda raza. Todos se vuelven ciudadanos al seguir el mismo procedimiento. Este libro es pàra que usted se guíe solito por todo ese procedimiento.

¿Cuales son los beneficios?

¿Por que debe hacerse uno ciudadano de los Estados Unidos? Sin duda, usted tiene sus buenas razones personales que lo hacen querer ser un ciudadano Americano. Pero, cualesquiera que sean, además de tener ud. sus razones personales, es buen idea darse cuenta de los muchos e importantes beneficios de la naturalización, o ciudadanía estadounidensa:

* Ud. va a poder votar en todas las elecciones.
* Ud. calificará para los trabajos que requieren la ciudadanía estadounidensa.
* Ud. les facilitará a sus parientes cercanos que viven en el extranjero el que se puedan inmigrar.
* Ud. ya no tendrá que cargar con su "mica" ni tendrá que notificarle al Servicio de Inmigración y Naturalización de su dirección.
* Ud. podrá obtener pasaporte que indica que es ciudadano Americano y posiblemente podrá viajar con más facilidad.

Chapter 1
ALL ABOUT NATURALIZATION

What is Naturalization?

Simply, "naturalization" means the becoming of a United States citizen by an alien. Congress has passed naturalization laws that set forth the conditions under which immigrants can become citizens. Such laws intend that an immigrant may become a citizen only if he or she is willing to accept the duties and responsibilities of citizenship and to preserve and protect American democracy. The laws are the same for men and women of all races. All become citizens by following the same procedure. This book is intended to guide you through those procedures, on your own.

What Are the Benefits?

Why become a United States citizen? You undoubtedly have some good personal reasons prompting your desire to become an American citizen. But in addition to your personal reasons, whatever they may be, it is a good idea to be aware of the many important benefits of naturalization, or United States citizenship:

* You will be able to vote in all elections.
* You will qualify for jobs that require United States citizenship.
* You will make immigration to the United States easier for your immediate relatives still abroad.
* You will no longer have to carry your alien registration card or notify the Immigration and Naturalization Service of your address.
* You will be able to obtain a passport indicating your American citizenship, possibly making travel easier. An American passport is often considered the most desirable to have.

El pasaporte Americano se considera, muchas veces, ser el más deseable.

* Ud. hasta podrá postularse para un puesto público con excepción a la presidencia o vice-presidencia de los Estados Unidos.

Es agradable saber que como ciudadano. ud. tambien puede compartir totalmente de las libertades del país con todos los beneficios y las responsabilidades que representa la ciudadanía.

¿Quién se puede naturalizar?

Las personas iguales a usted. Los extranjeros quienes se inmigran legalmente a los Estados Unidos, que deciden hacerse ciudadanos, y que pasan por el procedimiento de la naturalización. Entonces pueden disfrutar de los beneficios completos de la ciudadanía Americana junto con todos los ciudadanos que nacieron en los Estados Unidos.

Muchos millones de personas antes que usted de toda parte del mundo, de todas nacionalidades, creencias y colores han venido a los Estados Unidos a vivir. América...el crisol! Las razones personales de esta multitud que vino a radicar en los Estados Unidos y que se hicieron ciudadanos probablenente fueron tan variadas como las personas mismas. Solo podemos suponernos que todo inmigrante espera mejorar su vida al venir a vivir en América. La América se conoce extensamente como la "tierra de la oportunidad".

Antes de comenzar el procedimiento de la solicitud, es importante asegurar que usted reúne los requisitos que lo hacen elegible para solicitar.

¿Cuales son los requisitos para naturalizarse?

Antes de solicitar la naturalización, verifique el que usted reúna todo los ocho requerimientos generales que siguen:
1. Debe de tener al menos 18 años de edad.

* You can even run for public office, except that of President or Vice-President of the United States.

It is a nice feeling to know that as a citizen, you, too, can fully share in this country's freedoms, with all the benefits and responsibilities that citizenship entails.

Who Becomes Naturalized?

People like yourself. Aliens who legally immigrate to the United States, who choose to become citizens, and who go through the naturalization process. Then they may enjoy the full benefits of American citizenship right along with those citizens who were born in the United States.

Many millions of people before you, from all over the world, of all nationalities, creeds and colors have come to the United State to live. Because of this, it is no wonder that the expression "melting pot" evolved. America, the melting pot! The personal reasons for these multitudes settling in the United States and becoming citizens were probably as varied as the people themselves. We can only assume that all immigrants hope to better their lives by living in America. America is widely known also as the "land of opportunity."

Before beginning the application process, it is important to make sure that you meet the requirements making you eligible to apply.

What Are the Requirements for Naturalization?

Before you apply for naturalization, check to see that you meet all eight of the following general requirements:
1. You must be at least 18 years old.
2. You must have been lawfully admitted into the United States for permanent residence.
3. You must have lived in the United States continuously for at least 5 years, not counting short trips outside the U.S.A. Also, you must have resided for six

2. Debe de haber sido admitido legalmente a los Estados
   Unidos con residencia permanente.

3. Debe de haber vivido en los Estados Unidos constantemente
   por un mínimo de 5 años, sin contar viajes cortos afuera
   de los E.U.A. para ser elegible a solicitar la
   ciudadanía. Tambien, debe de haber vivido por 6 meses en
   el Estado adonde inicia su petición.

   Hay algunas excepciones importantes a éste
   requerimiento de residencia. Una excepción es el estar
   casado con un(a) esposo(a) ciudadano(a). ésto puede
   cortar el requerimiento de residencia a 3 años. Otras
   excepciones se hacen para ciertos (as) esposos(as) de
   ciudadanos(as) empleados(as) en el extranjero y para los
   miembros de las furerzas armadas de los Estados Unidos
   que sean extranjeros. Véase el Apéndice 1, "Las
   Excepciones Para Residencia Y Los Requisitos de
   Presencia Física" para los detalles sobre éstas
   excepciones y tambien los reglamentos sobre las
   vacaciones. Ejemplares de los formularios N-470 y N-426
   aparecen en el Apéndice 1 tambien. Se usan por ciertos
   individuos en casos especiales para llenar los
   requerimientos de residencia. Todavía otras excepciones
   al requerimiento de una residencia de 5 años se aplican
   a ciertos grupos de refugiados bajo lo que se llama la
   provisión "rollback". Para conocer más sobre esto. véase
   el Apéndice 2, "La Provisión "Rollback" Y los Requisitos
   de Residencia".

4. Debe de mostrar una reputación honrada y debe de creer en
   los principios de la Constitución de los Estados Unidos.
   Véase el Apéndice 3, "Reputación y Lealtad" para lo
   específico sobre éste requerimiento.

5. Debe de no haber pertenecido al partido Comunista por
   diez años antes de iniciar su solicitud, "La Petición
   para Naturalización".

6. No debe de haber quebrado cualquier ley de inmigración ni
   de haber recibido una orden para salir de los Estados
   Unidos.

7. Debe de poder hablar, comprender, leer y escribir un
   inglés sencillo, y tiene que pasar un examen sobre la
   historia y el gobierno de los Estados Unidos.

months in the state where you file your petition.

There are some important exceptions to this residency requirement. One exception is marriage to a citizen spouse, which can shorten the residency requirement to 3 years. Other exceptions are made for certain spouses of citizens employed abroad and for alien members of the United States armed forces. See Appendix 1, "Exceptions to Residence and Physical Presence Requirements" for details about these exceptions and also regulations about vacations. Samples of Forms N-470 and N-426 appear in Appendix 1, too. They are used by individuals in special cases to meet residency requirements. Still other exceptions to the 5 year residency requirement apply to certain refugee groups under what is called the "rollback" provision. For more on this, see Appendix 2, "The 'Rollback' Provision and Residency Requirements."

4. You must show good moral character and believe in the principals of the Constitution of the United States. See Appendix 3, "Character and Loyalty" for specifics on this requirement.

5. You must not have been a member of the Communist Party for ten years prior to filing your application, "Petition for Naturalization."

6. You must not have broken any immigration laws or have been ordered to leave the United States.

7. You must be able to speak, understand, read, and write simple English, and you must pass an examination about the history and government of the United States.

8. You must take an oath promising to give up your foreign allegiance, to obey the Constitution and laws of the United States, and to fight for the U.S.A. or do work of importance to the nation, if asked to do so.

Once you think you meet these 8 general requirements, you are ready to begin the first three steps in the naturalization process. So, onward to Chapter 2, **The Application**, which is your first step to United States citizenship.

8. Debe de haber tomado el juramento prometiendo entregar su
   fidelidad extranjera, obedecer la Constitución y las
   leyes de los Estado Unidos, y pelear por los E.U.A. ó
   hacer trabajo que le sea importante a la nación si se le
   pide hacerlo.

Luego que usted llene éstos 8 requerimientos generales,
estará listo para comenzar los primeros tres pasos en el
procedimiento de naturalización. Asi es que seguimos al Capítulo
2, **La Solicitud,** que es su primer paso hacia la ciudadanía de
los Estados Unidos.

World Wide Photos

Thousands Take Oath In Los Angeles Coliseum

Proud New Americans

Capitulo 2
LA SOLICITUD

El procedimiento entero de naturalización se cumple en tres pasos separados, el primero del cual es, que usted compléte y entrégue su solicitud. Esto se hace solamente despues de llenar los 8 requisitos generales que se anotan aqui inmediatamente arriba.

Cual formulario se debe usar

La "Solicitud para Iniciar la Petición para Naturalización", Formulario N-400 es el que usted usa si está solicitando su propia naturalización. El INS revisó éste formulario el 2 de mayo de 1982. Mientras que el INS aceptará los formularios de solicitud más 'viejos,' le valdría la pena obtener los más nuevos, ya que son más cortos y fáciles para llenar. Las instrucciones en éste libro son para el formulario más nuevo. La página una del Formulario N-400 enseña la fecha en la esquina izquierda de abajo adonde debe de leer: Formulario N-400 (Rev. 2-5-82).

Su solicitud consiste de tres cosas:
1. El Formulario N-400, "Solicitud para Iniciar la Petición de naturalización", la cual contiene cuatro páginas ademas de las intrucciones.
2. Una Carta de huellas digitales.
3. El Formulario G-325, "Informe Biográfico", una hoja que viene con su carbón para tener una cópia en duplicado. (G-325B tambien se usa si el servicio militar prévio es parte del antecedente del solicitante.)

El ejemplar 1, en éste capítulo, enseña a los fomularios N-400 y G-325 llenados, y se habla de una Carta de huellas digitales en las várias páginas despues. El N-400 es la solicitud básica, la que más seguidamente se le entrega al Servicio de Inmigración Y Naturalización(INS). Ya que se supone que los lectores de éste libro estarán usando el N-400, éste es el enfoque de nuestra atención. Cuando se usa ésta solicitud, es posible que los hijos

Chapter 2
THE APPLICATION

The entire naturalization process is accomplished in three separate steps, the first of which is for you to complete and submit your application. This is done only after meeting the 8 general requirements listed just above.

Which Application To Use

The "Application to File Petition for Naturalization," Form N-400, is the one you use if you are applying for your own naturalization. The INS revised this form on May 2, 1982. While the INS will accept the 'older' application forms, it might be worthwhile to obtain the latest ones, if only because it is shorter and easier to fill out. The instructions in this book are for the latest form. Page one of Form N-400 shows the date in the lower, left corner, where it should read: Form N-400 (Rev. 5-2-82).

Your application consists of three items:
1. Form N-400, "Application to File Petition for Naturalization," which is a four page form, plus instructions.
2. A fingerprint chart.
3. Form G-325, "Biographic Information," a sheet that comes with carbon paper for a duplicate copy. (G-325B is also to be used if previous military service is a part of the applicant's background.)

Sample I, in this chapter, shows Forms N-400 and G-325 filled out, and the fingerprint chart is discussed several pages below. N-400 is the basic application, the one most often submitted to the

menores automáticamente se hagan ciudadanos al mismo tiempo que los padres.

Incluyendo A Los Hijos Menores:

Si usted tiene hijos menores, debe de anotar a cada uno junto con algun dato o datos de cada uno, en las columnas "a" hasta el "h" del artículo 35 sobre la página tres de su solicitud, el Formulario N-400. Entonces se le es aconsejable escribir "DO"(Hágalo) en el artículo 36, el cual se le explica más adelante en ésta sección.

Estas son las reglas básicas referente a los menores tal como las explica el INS:

"Si un padre está solicitando su naturalización y espera estar naturalizado antes de que uno o más de sus hijos haya llegado a los 18 años de edad, es probable que dichos hijos que viven en los Estados Unidos se hagan automáticamente ciudadanos. Esto pasaría si el padre o la madre del hijo ya es ciudadano o si ha muerto, o si los dos padres estan legalmente separados y el padre que se esté naturalizando tiene la custodia legal de los hijos, o si la que se naturaliza es la madre del niño y éste niño nació sin el beneficio del matrimonio de sus padres."

No se les exigará a sus hijos que pasen los requisitos de la ciudadanía y del inglés para la naturalización, y un niño que tenga menos de la edad de 12 años tampoco tendrá que tomar el Juramento de Fidelidad.

Usted puede desear obtener un Certificado de Ciudadanía para cada hijo. Es buena idea ya que es una comprueba que se puede presentar a cualquier persona que quiera alzar alguna pregunta referente a su ciudadanía. Para obtener un Certificado de Ciudadanía para cada hijo, simplemente escriba "DO" en el artículo 36 de la página tres de su solicitud, el Formulario N-400. Entonces cuando entregue usted su propia solicitud, tambien incluya lo que sigue para cada hijo:

1. **El Honorario:** Adjunte un cheque o giro postal por la cantidad de $15, pagable al "Immigration and Naturalization Service" para cada hijo por quien usted desea tener un certificado.

Immigration and Naturalization Service (INS). Since it is presumed that readers of this book will be using the N-400, it is the focus of attention. When using this application, it is possible for minor children to automatically become citizens at the same time as the parent(s).

Including Minor Children:

If you have minor children, you are to list each, plus a few facts about them, in columns "a" through "h" of item #35 on page three of your application, Form N-400. Then it is advisable to write "DO" in item #36, which is explained later in this section.

Here are the basic rules regarding minors, as explained by the INS:

"If a parent who is applying for naturalization expects to be naturalized before one or more of his children reaches 18 years of age, it is likely that such children who are living in the United States automatically will become citizens. This would happen if the child's other parent already is a citizen, or is deceased, or if both parents are naturalized at the same time, or if the parents are legally separated and the parent being naturalized has the legal custody of the children, or if the parent being naturalized is the mother of the child and the child was born out of wedlock."

Your child(ren) will not be required to pass the citizenship and English requirements of naturalization nor will a child under age 14 have to take an Oath of Allegiance.

You may wish to obtain a Certificate of Citizenship for each child. This is a good idea since it is proof that can be presented to anyone who should ever raise a question as to his or her citizenship. To obtain a Certificate of Citizenship for each child, just write "DO" in item #36 on page three of your application, Form N-400. Then, when you submit your own application, also enclose the following for each child:

1. **Fee:** Enclose a check or money order for $15, made payable to "Immigration and Naturalization Service" for each child for whom a certificate is desired.
2. **Personal Description Form:** Complete Form N-604 for each child. See Sample 2 in this chapter.

Sample 1 - Form N-400
Application to File Petition for Naturalization

UNITED STATES DEPARTMENT OF JUSTICE
IMMIGRATION AND NATURALIZATION SERVICE

OMB NO. 1115-0009
Approval Expires 1/31/84

FEE STAMP

APPLICATION TO FILE PETITION FOR NATURALIZATION

Mail or take to:
IMMIGRATION AND NATURALIZATION SERVICE

ALIEN REGISTRATION
(Show the exact spelling of your name as it appears on your alien registration receipt card, and the number of your card. If you did not register, so state.)

Name Garcia-Gonzalez, Pedro

No. A55 416 038

(See INSTRUCTIONS. BE SURE YOU UNDERSTAND EACH QUESTION BEFORE YOU ANSWER IT. PLEASE PRINT OR TYPE.)

Section of Law .... (Leave Blank)

Date: Mar. 3, 1983

(1) My full true and correct name is...... Pedro Garcia-Gonzalez
(Full true name without abbreviations)

(2) I now live at...... 621 E. Emmett St.,
(Number and street,)
Santa Ana, Orange Co., California 92707
(City, county, state, zip code)

(3) I was born on...... Dec. 3, 1940 in San Pulco, Zacatecas, Mexico
(Month) (Day) (Year)   (City or town)   (County, province, or state)   (Country)

(4) I request that my name be changed to...... Pete Garcia

(5) Other names I have used are: none
(Include maiden name)

Sex: ☒ Male   ☐ Female

(6) Was your father or mother ever a United States citizen? .... ☐ Yes ☒ No
(If "Yes", explain fully)

(7) Can you read and write English? .... ☒ Yes ☐ No
(8) Can you speak English? .... ☒ Yes ☐ No
(9) Can you sign your name in English? .... ☒ Yes ☐ No

(10) My lawful admission for permanent residence was on...... March 14, 1963 ......under the name of
Garcia-Gonzalez, Pedro   (Month) (Day) (Year)
at San Ysidro, California
(City)   (State)

(11) (a) I have resided continuously in the United States since ...... March 14, 1963
(Month) (Day) (Year)

(b) I have resided continuously in the State of ...... California ...... since Mar. 14, 1963
(Month) (Day) (Year)

(c) During the last five years I have been physically in the United States for a total of ...... 60 ...... months.

(12) Do you intend to reside permanently in the United States? ☒ Yes ☐ No If "No," explain:

(13) In what places in the United States have you lived during the last 5 years? List present address FIRST.

FROM -	TO -	STREET ADDRESS	CITY AND STATE
(a) Feb. , 19 78	PRESENT TIME	621 E. Emmett St.	Santa Ana, California
(b) , 19	, 19		
(c) , 19	, 19		
(d) , 19	, 19		

(14) (a) Have you been out of the United States since your lawful admission as a permanent resident? .... ☐ Yes ☒ No
If "Yes" fill in the following information for every absence of *less than 6 months*, no matter how short it was.

DATE DEPARTED	DATE RETURNED	NAME OF SHIP, OR OF AIRLINE, RAILROAD COMPANY, BUS COMPANY, OR OTHER MEANS USED TO RETURN TO THE UNITED STATES	PLACE OR PORT OF ENTRY THROUGH WHICH YOU RETURNED TO THE UNITED STATES

(b) Since your lawful admission, have you been out of the United States for a period of 6 *months or longer*? .... ☐ Yes ☒ No
If "No", state "None"; If "Yes", fill in following information for every absence of more than 6 months.

DATE DEPARTED	DATE RETURNED	NAME OF SHIP OR OF AIRLINE, RAILROAD COMPANY, BUS COMPANY, OR OTHER MEANS USED TO RETURN TO THE UNITED STATES	PLACE OR PORT OF ENTRY THROUGH WHICH YOU RETURNED TO THE UNITED STATES
none			

Form N-400 (Rev. 5-2-82) Y

(1)

(OVER)

(15) The law provides that you may not be regarded as qualified for naturalization, if you knowingly committed certain offenses or crimes, even though you may not have been arrested. Have you ever, in or outside the United States:

    (*a*) knowingly committed any crime for which you have not been arrested? .... ☐ Yes   ☒ No

    (*b*) been arrested, cited, charged, indicted, convicted, fined or imprisoned for breaking or violating any law or ordinance, including traffic regulations? .... ☐ Yes   ☒ No

    If you answer "Yes" to (*a*) or (*b*), give the following information as to each incident.

	WHEN	WHERE	(City)	(State)	(Country)	NATURE OF OFFENSE	OUTCOME OF CASE, IF ANY
(*a*)							
(*b*)							
(*c*)							
(*d*)							
(*e*)							

(16) List your present and past membership in or affiliation with every organization, association, fund, foundation, party, club, society or similar group in the United States or in any other country or place, and your foreign military service. (If none, write "None.")

(*a*)	None		
(*b*)		, 19........	to 19........
(*c*)		, 19........	to 19........
(*d*)		, 19........	to 19........
(*e*)		, 19........	to 19........
(*f*)		, 19........	to 19........
(*g*)		, 19........	to 19........

(17) (*a*) Are you now, or have you ever, in the United States or in any other place, been a member of, or in any other way connected or associated with the Communist Party? (If "Yes", attach full explanation) .... ☐ Yes   ☒ No

    (*b*) Have you ever knowingly aided or supported the Communist Party directly, or indirectly through another organization, group or person? (If "Yes", attach full explanation) .... ☐ Yes   ☒ No

    (*c*) Do you now or have you ever advocated, taught, believed in, or knowingly supported or furthered the interests of Communism? (If "Yes", attach full explanation) .... ☐ Yes   ☒ No

(18) During the period March 23, 1933 to May 8, 1945, did you serve in, or were you in any affiliated with, either directly or indirectly, any military unit, paramilitary unit, police unit, self-defense unit, vigilante unit, citizen unit, unit of the Nazi Party or SS, government agency or office, extermination camp, concentration camp, prisoner of war camp, prison, labor camp, detention camp or transit camp, under the control of or affiliated with:

    (a) the Nazi Government of Germany .... ☐ Yes   ☒ No

    (b) any Government in any area occupied by, allied with, or established with the assistance or cooperation of, the Nazi Government of Germany? .... ☐ Yes   ☒ No

(19) During the period March 23, 1933 to May 8, 1945, did you ever order, incite, assist, or otherwise participate in the persecution of any person because of race, religion, national origin, or political opinion? .... ☐ Yes   ☒ No

(20) Have you borne any hereditary title or have you been of any order of nobility in any foreign state? .... ☐ Yes   ☒ No

(21) Have you ever been declared legally incompetent or have you ever been confined as a patient in a mental institution? .... ☐ Yes   ☒ No

(22) Are deportation proceedings pending against you, or have you ever been deported or ordered deported, or have you ever applied for suspension of deportation? .... ☐ Yes   ☒ No

(23) (*a*) My last Federal income tax return was filed 1982 (year) Do you owe any Federal taxes? .... ☐ Yes   ☒ No

    (*b*) Since becoming a permanent resident of the United States, have you:

    —filed an income tax return as a nonresident? .... ☐ Yes   ☒ No

    —failed to file an income tax return because you regarded yourself as a nonresident? .... ☐ Yes   ☒ No

    (If you answer "Yes" to (*a*) or (*b*) explain fully.)

(24) Have you ever claimed in writing, or in any other way, to be a United States citizen? .... ☐ Yes   ☒ No

(25) (*a*) Have you ever deserted from the military, air, or naval forces of the United States? .... ☐ Yes   ☒ No

    (*b*) If male, have you ever left the United States to avoid being drafted into the Armed Forces of the United States? ...... ☐ Yes   ☒ No

(26) The law provides that you may not be regarded as qualified for naturalization, if, at *any* time during the period for which you are required to prove good moral character, you have been a habitual drunkard; advocated or practiced polygamy; have been a prostitute or procured anyone for prostitution; have knowingly and for gain helped any alien to enter the United States illegally; have been an illicit trafficker in narcotic drugs or marijuana; have received your income mostly from illegal gambling, or have given false testimony for the purpose of obtaining any benefits under this Act. Have you ever, *anywhere*, been such a person or committed any of these acts? (If you answer yes to any of these, attach full explanation.) .... ☐ Yes   ☒ No

(27) Do you believe in the Constitution and form of government of the United States? .... ☒ Yes   ☐ No

(28) Are you willing to take the full oath of allegiance to the United States? (See Instructions) .... ☒ Yes   ☐ No

(29) If the law requires it, are you willing:

    (*a*) to bear arms on behalf of the United States? (If "No", attach full explanation) .... ☒ Yes   ☐ No

    (*b*) to perform noncombatant services in the Armed Forces of the United States? (If "No", attach full explanation) ..... ☒ Yes   ☐ No

    (*c*) to perform work of national importance under civilian direction? (If "No", attach full explanation) .... ☒ Yes   ☐ No

(30) (*a*) If male, did you ever register under United States Selective Service laws or draft laws? .... ☐ Yes   ☒ No

    If "Yes" give date ....; Selective Service No. ....; Local Board No. N/A ......; Present classification................

    (*b*) Did you ever apply for exemption from military service because of alienage, conscientious objections, or other reasons? ☐ Yes   ☒ No

    If "Yes," explain fully................

Not applicable

(31) If serving or ever served in the Armed Forces of the United States, give branch...;
from......................., 19......... to..., 19......., and from........................., 19......... to ...., 19.........
☐ inducted or ☐ enlisted at../...; Service No...;
type of discharge...; rank at discharge..
        (Honorable, Dishonorable, etc.)
reason for discharge...
                                              (alienage, conscientious objector, other)
☐ Reserve or ☐ National Guard from.. 19......... to..
(32) My occupation is...... Gardener

List the names, addresses, and occupations (or types of business) of your employers during the last 5 years. (If none, write "None.")
List present employment FIRST.

FROM-	TO-	EMPLOYER'S NAME	ADDRESS	OCCUPATION OR TYPE OF BUSINESS
(a) ...Jan., 19 78	PRESENT TIME	Fairroad Landscape Inc.	991 Manitoba Corona, Calif.	Gardener
(b) ...., 19......	.............., 19......			
(c) ...., 19......	.............., 19......			
(d) ...., 19......	.............., 19......			

(33) Complete this block if you are or have been married.
I am...... married .... The first name of my husband or wife is (was) ...... Laura
        (Separated, married, divorced, widowed)
We were married on...... 1-26-80 ......at...... Corona, Calif. ......He or she was born at...... Ensenada,
...... Mexico ......on .... He or she entered the United States at (place)...... San Ysidro
California...... on (date)...... 2-28-81 ......for permanent residence and now resides ☒ with me
☐ apart from me at ....(Show full address if living with you.)
He or she was naturalized on...... Not applicable ......at................................; Certificate No.............................,
or became a citizen by .... His or her Alien Registration No. is...... A13 691 385

(34) How many times have you been married?...1.... How many times has your husband or wife been married?...1.... If either of you has
been married more than once, fill in the following information for each previous marriage.

DATE MARRIED	DATE MARRIAGE ENDED	NAME OF PERSON TO WHOM MARRIED	SEX	(Check One) PERSON MARRIED WAS CITIZEN ☐ ALIEN ☐		HOW MARRIAGE ENDED
(a) none				☐	☐	
(b)				☐	☐	
(c)				☐	☐	
(d)				☐	☐	

(35) I have...1....children: (Complete columns (a) to (h) as to each child. If child lives with you, state "with me" in column (h), other-
        (Number)   wise give city and State of child's residence.)

(a) Given Names	(b) Sex	(c) Place Born (Country)	(d) Date Born	(e) Date of Entry	(f) Port of Entry	(g) Alien Registration No.	(h) Now Living at-
Enrique	M	Mexico	12-30-80	2-28-81	San Ysidro	A13 691 386	with me

(36) READ INSTRUCTION NO. 6 BEFORE ANSWERING QUESTION (36)

I...... do ......want certificates of citizenship for those of my children who are in the U.S. and are under age 18 years that are named below.
    (Do)   (Do Not)

(Enclose $15 for each child for whom you want certificates, otherwise, send no money with this application.)
...... Enrique Garcia
......................................(Write names of children under age 18 years and who are in the U.S. for whom you want certificates)

If present spouse is not the parent of the children named above, give parent's name, date and place of naturalization, and number of marriages.

...... Not applicable

(4)

Signature of person preparing form, if other than applicant.	SIGNATURE OF APPLICANT
I declare that this document was prepared by me at the request of applicant and is based on all information of which I have any knowledge. SIGNATURE	*Pedro Garcia – Gonzalez*
	ADDRESS AT WHICH APPLICANT RECEIVES MAIL
	621 E. Emmett St., Santa Ana, California
ADDRESS: DATE:	92707
	APPLICANT'S TELEPHONE NUMBER none

TO APPLICANT: DO NOT FILL IN BLANKS BELOW THIS LINE.

NOTE CAREFULLY.—This application must be sworn to before an officer of the Immigration and Naturalization Service at the time you appear before such officer for examination on this application.

AFFIDAVIT

I do swear that I know the contents of this application comprising pages 1 to 4, inclusive, and the supplemental forms thereto, No(s). ...., subscribed to by me; that the same are true to the best of my knowledge and belief; that corrections numbered ( ) to ( ) were made by me or at my request; and that this application was signed by me with my full, true, and correct name, SO HELP ME GOD.

Subscribed and sworn to before me by applicant at the preliminary investigation ( ) at ....

this .... day of ...., 19.......
I certify that before verification the above applicant stated in my presence that he/she had (heard) read the foregoing application, corrections therein and supplemental form(s) and understood the contents thereof.

....
(Complete and true signature of applicant)

....
(Naturalization examiner)

....
(For demonstration of applicant's ability to write English)

Non Filed ....

....
(Date, Reasons)

NOTICE TO APPLICANTS:

Authority for collection of the information requested on this form and those forms mentioned in the instructions thereto is continued in Sections 328, 329, 332, 334, 335 or 341 of the Immigration and Nationality Act of 1952 (8 U.S.C. 1439, 1440, 1443, 1445, 1446 or 1452). Submission of the information is voluntary inasmuch as the immigration and nationality laws of the United States do not require an alien to apply for naturalization. If your Social Security number is omitted from a form, no right, benefit or privilege will be denied for your failure to provide such number. However, as military records are indexed by such numbers, verification of your military service, if required to establish eligibility for naturalization, may prove difficult. The principal purposes for soliciting the information are to enable designated officers of the Immigration and Naturalization Service to determine the admissibility of a petitioner for naturalization and to make appropriate recommendations to the naturalization courts. All or any part of the information solicited may, as a matter of routine use, be disclosed to a court exercising naturalization jurisdiction and to other federal, state, local or foreign law enforcement or regulatory agencies, Department of Defense, including any component thereof, the Selective Service System, the Department of State, the Department of the Treasury, Central Intelligence Agency, Interpol and individuals and organizations in the processing of the application or petition for naturalization, or during the course of investigation to elicit further information required by the Immigration and Naturalization Service to carry out its function. Information solicited which indicates a violation or potential violation of law, whether civil, criminal or regulatory in nature may be referred, as routine use, to the appropriate agency, whether federal, state, local or foreign, charged with the responsibility of investigating, enforcing or prosecuting such violations. Failure to provide any or all of the solicited information may result in an adverse recommendation to the court as to an alien's eligibility for naturalization and denial by the court of a petition for naturalization.

For sale by the Superintendent of Documents, U.S. Government Printing Office
Washington, D.C. 20402

U.S. GOVERNMENT PRINTING OFFICE : 1982 O—371-136

Sample 2 - Form N-604
Child's Personal Description Form

UNITED STATES DEPARTMENT OF JUSTICE
Immigration and Naturalization Service

Form Approved
OMB No. 43-R0474

TO BE COMPLETED IF YOU ARE APPLYING FOR NATURALIZATION AND WANT A CERTIFICATE OF CITIZENSHIP FOR YOUR
CHILD *(READ INSTRUCTIONS ON REVERSE SIDE CAREFULLY)*

Name of Child __Enrique Garcia-Sanchez__

Address of Child __621 E. Emmett St. Santa Ana, Calif.__
                                                    92707

Alien Registration Number   A-__13 691 386__

CHILD'S PERSONAL DESCRIPTION FORM
(Type or Print)

Sex __M__ ; date of birth __12-30-80__ ; country of birth __Mexico__

complexion __Light__ ; color of eyes __brown__ ; color of hair __brown__

height __3__ feet __1__ inches; weight __60__ pounds; visible distinctive marks __none__

_____ ; marital status __single__

Issue child's certificate in the name of: __Enrique Garcia__

Form N—604
(Rev.6—15—79)N

(OVER)

28

Form G-325: Biographical Information

U.S. Department of Justice
Immigration and Naturalization Service

BIOGRAPHIC INFORMATION

OMB No. 1115-0066
Approval expires 4-30-85

(Family name) (First name) (Middle name)	☒ MALE ☐ FEMALE	BIRTHDATE(Mo.-Day-Yr.) 12-3-40	NATIONALITY Mexican	FILE NUMBER A55 416 038
GARCIA-GONZALEZ, Pedro				

ALL OTHER NAMES USED (Including names by previous marriages) None	CITY AND COUNTRY OF BIRTH San Pulco, Mexico	SOCIAL SECURITY NO. (If any) 566069565

	FAMILY NAME FIRST NAME DATE, CITY AND COUNTRY OF BIRTH(If known)	CITY AND COUNTRY OF RESIDENCE.
FATHER	Garcia, Roberto, 1-12-20, San Pulco, Mexico,	Deceased
MOTHER (Maiden name)	Gonzalez, Maria, 12-3-21, San Pulco, Mexico	San Pulco, Mexico

HUSBAND (If none, so state) OR WIFE FAMILY NAME (For wife, give maiden name)	FIRST NAME	BIRTHDATE	CITY & COUNTRY OF BIRTH	DATE OF MARRIAGE	PLACE OF MARRIAGE
Sanchez	Laura	1-12-50	Ensenada Mexico	1-26-80	Corona, Calif. USA

FORMER HUSBANDS OR WIVES (if none, so state) FAMILY NAME (For wife, give maiden name)	FIRST NAME	BIRTHDATE	DATE & PLACE OF MARRIAGE	DATE AND PLACE OF TERMINATION OF MARRIAGE
None				

APPLICANT'S RESIDENCE LAST FIVE YEARS. LIST PRESENT ADDRESS FIRST.

STREET AND NUMBER	CITY	PROVINCE OR STATE	COUNTRY	FROM MONTH	YEAR	TO MONTH	YEAR
621 E. Emmet St.	Santa Ana	California	USA	Feb.	78	PRESENT TIME	

APPLICANT'S LAST ADDRESS OUTSIDE THE UNITED STATES OF MORE THAN ONE YEAR

STREET AND NUMBER	CITY	PROVINCE OR STATE	COUNTRY	FROM MONTH	YEAR	TO MONTH	YEAR
222 Aquiles Serdan	San Pulco	Zacatecas	Mexico	12	40	2	63

APPLICANT'S EMPLOYMENT LAST FIVE YEARS. (IF NONE, SO STATE.) LIST PRESENT EMPLOYMENT FIRST

FULL NAME AND ADDRESS OF EMPLOYER	OCCUPATION (SPECIFY)	FROM MONTH	YEAR	TO MONTH	YEAR
Fairroad Landscape Inc.	Gardener	Jan.	78	PRESENT TIME	

Show below last occupation abroad if not shown above. (Include all information requested above.)

Self-employed, San Pulco, Zacatecas, Mexico	Farmer	12	59	2	63

THIS FORM IS SUBMITTED IN CONNECTION WITH APPLICATION FOR:	SIGNATURE OF APPLICANT	DATE
☒ NATURALIZATION ☐ OTHER (SPECIFY): ☐ STATUS AS PERMANENT RESIDENT	*Pedro Garcia-Gonzalez*	
Are all copies legible? ☒ Yes	IF YOUR NATIVE ALPHABET IS IN OTHER THAN ROMAN LETTERS, WRITE YOUR NAME IN YOUR NATIVE ALPHABET IN THIS SPACE:	

PENALTIES: SEVERE PENALTIES ARE PROVIDED BY LAW FOR KNOWINGLY AND WILLFULLY FALSIFYING OR CONCEALING A MATERIAL FACT.

APPLICANT: BE SURE TO PUT YOUR NAME AND ALIEN REGISTRATION NUMBER IN THE BOX OUTLINED BY HEAVY BORDER BELOW.

COMPLETE THIS BOX (Family name)	(Given name)	(Middle name)	(Alien registration number)
GARCIA-GONZALEZ, Pedro		A 55 416 038	

Form G-325 (Rev. 10-1-82) Y

(1) **Ident.**

2. **Formulario de Descripción Personal**: Complete el
   Formulario N-604 para cada hijo. Véase el ejemplar 2.
3. **Documentación**: Incluya documentos adjuntos como se lo
   exige el artículo 6 en las "Intrucciones para el
   Solicitante" que viene junto con su Formulario N-400.
4. **Fotografías**: Incluya tres fotos de cada hijo, tomadas
   dentro de los 30 días a partir de la fecha de la
   entrega de su solicitud, y escriba el Número de la
   "Mica" de su hijo levemente en lapíz atrás de sus
   fotos.

En ésta forma su hijo se hará ciudadano automáticamente en la
misma fecha que usted se naturaliza. Sin embargo sus hijos
recibirán sus Certificados de Ciudadanía por correo más tarde
del INS. Si, por alguna razón no se le expide el certificado, se
le reembolsará su honorario.

Solicitudes Para Clases Especiales:

Hay otras solicitudes para clases especiales de personas,
tal como el Formulario N-402, "Solicitud para Iniciar Peticiones
de Naturalización a Nombre de un Niño" y el Formulario N-600,
"Solicitud para Certificado de Ciudadanía". Ya que el N-400 es
el que usted estará usando con más probabilidad, sigue solo una
breve descripción y copias ejemplares de dos solicitudes.

El Formulario N-402 es la solicitud que se usará para la
naturalización de niños que no se vuelven automáticamente
ciudadanos a través de sus padres. Por ejemplo, si solo uno de
los padres del niño se naturaliza y el otro permanece como un
residente, el niño nó se vuelve automáticamente ciudadano.
Junto con ésta solicitud usted debe de entregar:
1. Un formulario de Informe Biográfico, G-325,
2. Una Carta de huellas digitales (solo si el níño tiene 14
   años o más).
3. Tres fotografías tomadas dentro de los 30 días a partir
   de la fecha en la cual se entregó la solicitud.

El tiempo es muy importante porque todos los tres pasos del
procedimiento de naturalización se deben de completar antes de
que cumpla el niño 18 años. En otras palabras, el niño debe de
ser admitido como ciudadano en la actualidad por un juez antes
de que cumpla los 18 años. Ya que el procedimiento de

3. **Documents:** include accompanying documents as required by item #6 in "Instructions to the Applicant" that comes with your Form N-400.

4. **Photographs:** Include three photographs of each child, taken within 30 days of the date your application is submitted, and write the child's Alien Registration Number lightly in pencil on the back of the pictures.

This way your child will become a citizen automatically on the same date that you are naturalized. However, the children will receive their Certificates of Citizenship at a later date by mail from the INS. If for any reason a certificate is not issued, the fee will be refunded.

Applications for Special Classes:

There are other applications for special classes of persons, such as Form N-402, "Application to File Petitions for Naturalization in Behalf of Child" and Form N-600, "Application for Certificate of Citizenship." Since the N-400 is the one you will most likely be using, only a brief description and sample copies of these two applications follow.

Form N-402 is the application to be used for the naturalization of children who do not become citizens automatically through their parent(s). For example, if only one of the child's parents becomes naturalized and the other remains a permanent resident, the child does not automatically become a citizen. Instead, the citizen parent of an alien child must complete Form N-402, which can be done at any time after the parent becomes a citizen. Along with this application you must submit:

1. a G-325 Biographic Information form,
2. a fingerprint chart (only if the child is age 14 or older),
3. Three photographs taken within 30 days of the date the application is submitted.

Timing is very important because all 3 steps of the naturalization process must be completed before the child's 18th birthday. In other words, the child must actually be admitted to citizenship by a judge, prior to becoming age 18. Because the naturalization process can take well over a year, plan to submit Form N-402 at least by the time your child is age 16, or better yet even sooner, if at all possible.

Sample 3 - Form N-402
Application on Behalf of a Child

UNITED STATES DEPARTMENT OF JUSTICE
IMMIGRATION AND NATURALIZATION SERVICE

Form approved.
OMB No. 43–R0081.

APPLICATION TO FILE PETITION FOR NATURALIZATION IN BEHALF OF CHILD
Under Section 322 of the Immigration and Nationality Act

Take or Mail to:
IMMIGRATION AND NATURALIZATION SERVICE.

CHILD's NAME AND ALIEN REGISTRATION NUMBER

Name Raymond Francois RANIERE

No. A 55 418 036

Date Mar. 3 , 19 83

I (We), the undersigned, desire that a petition for naturalization be filed in behalf of my (our) child in the
U.S. District Court at Los Angeles, California
(Name of court)   (City or town)   (State)

(1) My full, true, and correct name is Thomas Raniere
(Full, true name of citizen parent or citizen adoptive parent, without abbreviations)

(2) My present place of residence is 7751 Liberty Ave., Huntington Beach, California 92647
(Apt. No.) (Number and street) (City or town) (County) (State) (ZIP Code)

(3) I am a citizen of the United States of America and was born on Jan. 2, 1944 in Brooklyn, N.Y., USA
(Month) (Day) (Year)   (City, State, and Country)

(If not a native-born citizen) I was naturalized on Not applicable at
(Month) (Day) (Year)   (City and State)

certificate No. , or I became a citizen of the United States through

(Is the child's other parent a citizen of the United States?   ☐ Yes   ☐ No)

(Complete (1a) to (3a) only if second parent wishes to join in application)

(1a) My full, true, and correct name is Not applicable
(Full, true name of second citizen parent or citizen adoptive parent, without abbreviations)

(2a) My present place of residence is
(Apt. No.) (Number and street) (City or town) (County) (State) (ZIP Code)

(3a) I am a citizen of the United States of America and was born on in
(Month) (Day) (Year)   (City, State, and Country)

(If not a native-born citizen) I was naturalized on at
(Month) (Day) (Year)   (City and State)

certificate No. , or I became a citizen of the United States through

(4) I am (We are) the parent(s) of Raymond Francois RANIERE
(Full, true name of child, without abbreviations)
in whose behalf this application for naturalization is filed.

(5) The said child now resides with me (us) at 7751 Liberty Ave., Huntington Beach,
(Apt. No.) (Number and street) (City or town)

Orange, California 92647 is single and is a citizen, subject, or national of Netherlands
(County) (State) (ZIP Code)   (Married) (Single)

(6) The said child was born on Jan. 25, 1970 in The Hague, Netherlands
(Month) (Day) (Year)   (City and Country)

(7) The said child was lawfully admitted to the United States for permanent residence on May 3, 1977 at
(Month) (Day) (Year)

Los Angeles, California under the name of Raymond Francois Raniere
(City) (State)

on the Pan Am Air and does intend to reside permanently in the United States.
(Name of vessel or other means of conveyance)

(8) I (We) desire the naturalization court to change the name of the child to Raymond Francis Raniere
(Give full name desired, without abbreviations)

(9) If application is in behalf of an adopted child:
I (We) adopted said child on Jan. 3, 1975 in the The Hague Court
(Month) (Day) (Year)   (Name of court)

at The Hague, Netherlands before (s)he was 16 years of age.
(City or town) (State) (Country)

The said child has resided continuously in the United States with me (us) in my (our) legal custody since May 3, 1977
(Month) (Day) (Year)

(1)

32

(10) Since such child's lawful admission to the United States for permanent residence, (s)he has not been absent from the United States at any time except as follows (if none, state "None"):

DEPARTED FROM THE UNITED STATES			RETURNED TO THE UNITED STATES		
PORT	DATE (MONTH, DAY, YEAR)	VESSEL OR OTHER MEANS OF CONVEYANCE	PORT	DATE (MONTH, DAY, YEAR)	VESSEL OR OTHER MEANS OF CONVEYANCE
None					

(11) Has such child ever been a patient in a mental institution, or ever been treated for a mental illness? ☐ Yes ☒ No

(12) The law provides that a person may not be regarded as qualified for naturalization under certain conditions, if the person knowingly committed certain offenses or crimes, even though not arrested therefor. Has such child ever in or outside the United States:

   (a) Knowingly committed any crime for which (s)he has not been arrested? . . . . ☐ Yes ☒ No

   (b) Been arrested, charged with violation of any law or ordinance, summoned into court as a defendant, convicted, fined, imprisoned, or placed on probation or parole, or forfeited collateral for any act involving a crime, misdemeanor, or breach of any law or ordinance? . . . . ☐ Yes ☒ No

If the answer to (a) or (b) is "Yes," on a separate sheet, give the following information as to each incident: when and where occurred, offense involved, and outcome of case if any.

(13) Are deportation proceedings pending against such child or has such child ever been deported or ordered deported, or has such child ever applied for suspension of deportation or for preexamination? . . . . . . ☐ Yes ☐ No

(14) List the child's membership in every organization, association, fund, foundation, party, club, society, or similar group in the United States and in any other place, during the past ten years, and his foreign military service. (If none, write "None.")

(a) .... , 19......... to 19........... None
(b) .... , 19......... to 19...........
(c) .... , 19......... to 19...........
(d) .... , 19......... to 19...........

(15) Has such child ever served in the Armed Forces of the United States? . . . . ☐ Yes ☒ No

(16) (Answer only if the child is of an understanding age.) If the law requires it, is the child willing to bear arms or perform noncombatant service in the Armed Forces of the United States or perform work of national importance under civilian direction? If "No" explain fully on a separate sheet of paper . . . . ☒ Yes ☐ No

(17) Since the child's lawful admission to the United States for permanent residence, my wife (husband) and I have been absent from the United States as follows (if no absences, state "None"):

   None

(18) My wife (husband) and I have been married as follows (give information as to each marriage): (Use extra sheet of paper if necessary.)

DATE MARRIED	DATE MARRIAGE ENDED	NAME OF SPOUSE	HOW MARRIAGE ENDED (Death or divorce)
Dec. 12, 1974	N/A	Claire Weddik	N/A

(2)

33

Not applicable

(19) A petition for naturalization has .... heretofore been filed on behalf of said child on ....
                                    (not)   (Month) (Day) (Year)

at .... in .... and denied.
     (City)   (County)   (State)   (Name of court)

Thomas Ranière   _Claire Weddik_
      (Signature of 1st parent)   (Signature of 2d parent)

7751 Liberty Ave. Huntington Beach,   7751 Liberty Ave. Huntington Beach,
     (Address of 1st parent) Calif. 92647   (Address of 2d parent) Calif. 92647

(714) 100-9990   March 7, 1983   (714) 100-9990   March 7, 1983
(Telephone No.)   (Date)   (Telephone No.)   (Date)

SIGNATURE OF PERSON PREPARING FORM, IF OTHER THAN APPLICANT(S)

I declare that this document was prepared by me at the request of the applicant(s) and is based on all information of which I have any knowledge.

Hank Arman DuBois   200 Star Street, Suite 102   March 7, 1983
      (Signature)   Westminster, (Address) Calif. 92661   (Date)

TO APPLICANTS: DO NOT WRITE BELOW THESE LINES

AFFIDAVIT

I do swear (affirm) that I know the contents of this application comprising pages 1 to 3, inclusive, subscribed by me; that the same are true to the best of my knowledge and belief; that corrections number ( ) to ( ) were made by me or at my request; and that this application was signed by me with my full, true name, SO HELP ME GOD.

Subscribed and sworn (affirmed) to before me at the preliminary investigation (examination) at ....
this .... day of ...., 19........

I certify that before verification the parent(s) stated in my presence that he (she they) had .... read the
                                                                        (heard)
foregoing application and corrections therein and understood the contents thereof.

_____
(Complete and true signature of 1st parent)

_____
(Complete and true signature of 2d parent)

_____
(Naturalization Examiner)

(1st witness) .... Occupation ....

residing at ....
                  (Apt. No.)   (Street address, city or town, State and ZIP Code)

(2d witness) .... Occupation ....

residing at ....
                  (Apt. No.)   (Street address, city or town, State and ZIP Code)

U.S. .... Physical presence................................. months. .... (Naturalization Examiner)

Nonfiled ....
                  (Date, reason, and examiner's initials)

(3)   U.S. GOVERNMENT PRINTING OFFICE : 1979—O—279—665

34

Sample 4 - Form N-600
Application for Certificate of Citizenship

UNITED STATES DEPARTMENT OF JUSTICE
IMMIGRATION AND NATURALIZATION SERVICE

APPLICATION FOR CERTIFICATE OF CITIZENSHIP

FEE STAMP

Form approved
OMB No. 1115-0018

Take or mail this application to:
IMMIGRATION AND NATURALIZATION SERVICE

(Print or type) ___Maria Ulloa-Contreras___ nee ___same___
(Full, True Name, without Abbreviations)

Date ___Mar. 3, 1983___

(Maiden name, if any)

___1004 S. Standard___
(Apartment number, Street address, and, if appropriate, "in care of")

___Santa Ana, Orange, California 92701___
(City)   (County)   (State)   (ZIP Code)

___None___
(Telephone Number)

ALIEN REGISTRATION
No. ___None___

(SEE INSTRUCTIONS. BE SURE YOU UNDERSTAND EACH QUESTION BEFORE YOU ANSWER IT.)

I hereby apply to the Commissioner of Immigration and Naturalization for a certificate showing that I am a citizen of the United States of America.

(1) I was born in ___Mexicali, Baja California___ on ___4-11-59___
(City)   (State or country)   (Month) (Day) (Year)

(2) My personal description is: Sex ___F___ ; complexion ___Dark___ ; color of eyes ___Black___ ; color of hair ___Black___ ;
height ___5___ feet ___3___ inches; weight ___130___ pounds; visible distinctive marks ___None___
Marital status: ☒ Single; ☐ Married; ☐ Divorced; ☐ Widow(er).

(3) I arrived in the United States at • ___San Ysidro, California___ on ___9-7-69___
(City and State)   (Month) (Day) (Year)

under the name ___Maria Ulloa-Contreras___ by means of ___Car___
(Name of ship or other means of arrival)

☐ on U.S. Passport No. ___Not applicable___ issued to me at _____ on _____ ;
(Month) (Day) (Year)

☐ on an Immigrant Visa. ☒ Other (specify) ___Birth Certificate___

(4) FILL IN THIS BLOCK ONLY IF YOU ARRIVED IN THE UNITED STATES BEFORE JULY 1, 1924.

(a) My last permanent foreign residence was ___Not applicable___
(City)   (Country)

(b) I took the ship or other conveyance to the United States at _____
(City)   (Country)

(c) I was coming to _____ at _____
(Name of person in the United States)   (City and State where this person was living)

(d) I traveled to the United States with _____
(Names of passengers or relatives with whom you traveled, and their relationship to you, if any)

(5) Have you been out of the United States since you first arrived? ☐ Yes ☒ No. If "Yes" fill in the following information for every absence.

Date Departed	Date Returned	Name of Airline, or Other Means Used To Return to the United States	Port of Return to the United States

(6) I (have) (have not) filed a petition for naturalization.

(If "have", attach full explanation.)

TO THE APPLICANT.—Do not write between the double lines below. Continue on next page.

ARRIVAL RECORDS EXAMINED	ARRIVAL RECORD FOUND
Card index _____	Place _____ Date _____
Index books _____	Name _____
Manifests _____	
	Manner _____
	Marital status _____ Age _____
	(Signature of person making search)

Form N-600 (Rev. 1-31-81) Y   (1)

(CONTINUE HERE)

(7) I claim United States citizenship through my *(check whichever applicable)* ☒ father; ☐ mother; ☐ both parents;

☐ adoptive parent(s)   ☐ husband

(8) My father's name is _Roberto Ulloa_____; he was born on _5-16-27_____
                                                                   (Month) (Day) (Year)

at _Anaheim, California, USA_____; and resides at _551 River Rd. Corona, California_
     (City)   (State or country)   (Street address, city, and State or country. If dead, write

------------------- He became a citizen of the United States by ☐ birth; ☐ naturalization on _____
"dead" and date of death.)   (Month) (Day) (Year)

in the ___Not applicable_____ Certificate of Naturalization No. _____;
           (Name of court, city, and State)

☐ through his parent(s), and ____(was) (was not)____ issued Certificate of Citizenship No. A or AA _____

(If known) His former Alien Registration No. was _____

He (has) (has not) lost United States citizenship. *(If citizenship lost, attach full explanation.)*

He resided in the United States from ___1927___ to __1932__; from __1947__ to _present_ from _____ to _____;
                                       (Year)   (Year)   (Year)   (Year)   (Year)   (Year)

from _____ to _____; from _____ to _____; I am the child of his ___1st_____ marriage.
      (Year)   (Year)   (Year)   (Year)   (1st, 2d, 3d, etc.)

(9) My mother's present name is _Carolina Contreras-Ulloa_; her maiden name was _Carolina Contreras-Esparza_

she was born on __12-25-29_____; at __Guadalajara, Jalisco, Mexico_____; she resides
                 (Month) (Day) (Year)   (City)   (State or country)

at _551 River Rd. Corona, California_____ She became a citizen of the United States
     (Street address, city, and State or country. If dead, write "dead" and date of death.)

by ☐ birth; ☐ naturalization under the name of _____Not applicable_____

on _____ in the _____
    (Month) (Day) (Year)   (Name of court, city, and State)

Certificate of Naturalization No. _____; ☐ through her parent(s), and __(was) (was not)__ issued Certificate

of Citizenship No. A or AA _____ (If known) Her former Alien Registration No. was _____

She (has) (has not) lost United States citizenship. *(If citizenship lost, attach full explanation.)*

She resided in the United States from _____ to _____; from _____ to _____; from _____ to _____; from _____
                                      (Year)   (Year)   (Year)   (Year)   (Year)   (Year)   (Year)

to _____; from _____ to _____; I am the child of her _____ marriage.
   (Year)   (Year)   (Year)   (1st, 2d, etc.)

(10) My mother and my father were married to each other on __6-14-55__ at _Mexicali, Baja Calif. Mexico_
                                                              (Month) (Day) (Year)   (City)   (State or country)

(11) If claim is through adoptive parent(s):
     I was adopted on _____Not applicable_____ in the _____
                          (Month) (Day) (Year)   (Name of Court)

at _____ before I was 16 years of age by my _____
     (City or town)   (State)   (Country)   (mother, father, parents)

(12) My (father) (mother) served in the Armed Forces of the United States from __Not applicable_____
                                                                                    (Date)

to _____ and _(was) (was not)__ honorably discharged.
        (Date)

(13) I (have) (have not) lost my United States citizenship. *(If citizenship lost, attach full explanation.)*

(14) I submit the following documents with this application:

Nature of Document	Names of Persons Concerned
Birth Certificate	Applicant (Maria Ulloa-Contreras)
Marriage Certificate	Parents (Roberto & Carolina Ulloa)
Birth Certificate	Father (Roberto Ulloa)

(2)

(15) Fill in this block if your brother, sister, mother or father ever applied to the Immigration Service for a certificate of citizenship.   Not applicable

NAME OF RELATIVE	RELATIONSHIP	Date of Birth	WHEN APPLICATION SUBMITTED	CERTIFICATE NO. AND FILE NO., IF KNOWN, AND LOCATION OF OFFICE

(16) Fill in this block only if you are now or ever have been a married woman. I have been married .... time(s), as follows: Not applicable
(1, 2, 3, etc.)

DATE MARRIED	NAME OF HUSBAND	CITIZENSHIP OF HUSBAND	If MARRIAGE HAS BEEN TERMINATED:	
			Date Marriage Ended	How Marriage Ended (*Death or divorce*)

(17) Fill in this block only if you claim citizenship through a husband. (*Marriage must have occurred prior to September 22, 1922.*)   Not applicable

Name of citizen husband .... ; he was born on ....
(Give full and complete name)   (Month) (Day) (Year)

at .... ; and resides at ....
(City)   (State or country)   (Street address, city, and State or country. If dead, write

He became a citizen of the United States by ☐ birth; ☐ naturalization on ....
"dead" and date of death.)   (Month) (Day) (Year)

in the .... Certificate of Naturalization No. .... ;
(Name of court, city, and State)

☐ through his parent(s), and ..(was).. ..(was not).. issued Certificate of Citizenship No. A or AA ....

He ..(has).. ..(has not).. since lost United States citizenship. (*If citizenship lost, attach full explanation.*)

I am of the .... race. Before my marriage to him, he was married .... time(s), as follows:
(1, 2, 3, etc.)

DATE MARRIED	NAME OF WIFE	If MARRIAGE HAS BEEN TERMINATED:	
		Date Marriage Ended	How Marriage Ended (*Death or divorce*)

(18) Fill in this block only if you claim citizenship through your stepfather. (*Applicable only if mother married U.S. Citizen prior to September 22, 1922.*)

The full name of my stepfather is .... Not applicable .... ; he was born on ....
(Month) (Day) (Year)

at .... ; and resides at ....
(City)   (State or country)   (Street address, city, and State or country. If dead, write

He became a citizen of the United States by ☐ birth; ☐ naturalization on ....
"dead" and date of death.)   (Month) (Day) (Year)

in the .... Certificate of Naturalization No. .... ;
(Name of court, city, and State)

☐ through his parent(s), and ..(was).. ..(was not).. issued Certificate of Citizenship No. A or AA ....

He ..(has).. ..(has not).. since lost United States citizenship. (*If citizenship lost, attach full explanation.*)

He and my mother were married to each other on .... at ....
(Month) (Day) (Year)   (City and State or country)

My mother is of the .... race. She ..(was).. ..(was not).. issued Certificate of Citizenship No. A ....

Before marrying my mother, my stepfather was married .... time(s), as follows:
(1, 2, 3, etc.)

DATE MARRIED	NAME OF WIFE	If MARRIAGE HAS BEEN TERMINATED:	
		Date Marriage Ended	How Marriage Ended (*Death or divorce*)

(19) I ..(have).. ((have not)) previously applied for a certificate of citizenship on ---------------, at ----------------------
(Date)   (Office)

(20) Signature of person preparing form, if other than applicant. I declare that this document was prepared by me at the request of the applicant and is based on all information of which I have any knowledge.

SIGNATURE:

ADDRESS: DATE:

(SIGN HERE) *Maria Ulloa-Contreras*
(Signature of applicant or parent or guardian)

(3)

37

naturalización puede tomar bastante más que un año, planée
entregar el Formulario N-402 al menos cuando su niño tenga 16
años, y si le es posible, sería mejor si fuera más pronto.

El ejemplar 3 enseña el Formulario N-402, "Solicitud para
Iniciar una Petición de Naturalización a Nombre de un Niño".
Para más informe referente a cuando se debe de usar ésta
solicitud, consulte el folleto, **Formulario N-17**, "Los
Requerimientos de Naturalización e Informe General", y en
particular, la sección de "Naturalización para Niños ". Para
obtener uno de éstos folletos gratis, refiérase a la siguiente
sección aqui abajo, **Adonde Obtener Una Solicitud**.

El Formulario N-600 es para las personas que ya son
ciudadanos a través de otra persona, tal como el marido o el
padre, pero que desean un certificado para enseñár una comprueba
de ciudadanía. Las circunstancias son muy variables en casos de
ciudadanía por "adquisición", pero si usted piensa que ya es
ciudadano de los Estados Unidos a través de su esposo o padre,
entonces llene el Formulario N-600 para solicitar su Certificado
de Ciudadanía. Si no está muy seguro, entonces sería mejor
buscar primero a un consejero experto de cualquier oficina del
INS o a un abogado de Inmigración antes de entregar su
solicitud.

El Fomulario N-600 puede ser iniciado por un solicitante
adulto, o puede ser iniciado por un padre ó tutor a nombre de un
niño. No se le exige que se inicie ésta solicitud del todo. Es
entéramente voluntario, y la falta de entregar un N-600 no
afecta en ninguna forma la ciudadanía de una persona. Un
honorario de $15.00 se tiene que entregar junto con la
solicitud, y nó se le devolverá no importa que acción se tome
sobre la solicitud. Además del honorario, usted debe de entregar
junto con su solicitud, tres fotos y cualquier comprueba de
nacimiento, muerte, divorcio, adopción y otras cosas esenciales
en forma de cetificado o documentos para comprobar su reclamo a
la ciudadanía a través del matrimonio o de los padres.

Para sumar, la mayoría de las personas, al cumplir con los 8
requisitos de naturalización, usarán el Fomulario N-400,

Sample 3 shows Form N-402, "Application to File Petition for Naturalization in Behalf of Child." For more information regarding when to use this application, consult the pamphlet **Form N-17,** "Naturalization Requirements and General Information," particularly the section "Naturalization of Children." To obtain one of these free pamphlets, refer to the next section below, **Where To Get An Application.**

Form N-600 is for persons who are already citizens through someone else, like a husband or parent, but desire a certificate to show proof of their citizenship. The circumstances vary greatly in cases of citizenship through "acquisition," but if you think that you are already a citizen of the United States through a spouse or parent, then fill out Form N-600 to apply for your Certificate of Citizenship. If you are not at all sure, it would be best to first seek expert advice from any INS office or an immigration attorney before submitting this application.

Form N-600 can be filed by an adult applicant, or it can be filed by a parent or guardian on behalf of a child. It is not required to file this application at all. It is an entirely voluntary matter, and failure to submit an N-600 does not in any way affect a person's citizenship. A fee of $15.00 must be submitted along with the application, and it will not be refunded regardless of the action taken on the application. In addition to this fee, you must also submit with your application the usual three photographs and any evidence of birth, marriage, death, divorce, adoption, and other essential matters in the form of certificates or documents to prove your claim to citizenship through marriage or parents.

In summary, the majority of people, having met the 8 general requirements for naturalization, will use Form N-400, "Application to File Petition for Naturalization." If you think you may need some other application for your special case, contact your nearest INS office and ask. This way, you will be absolutely certain to acquire the correct application right from the start.

"Solicitud para Iniciar la Petición de Naturalización". Si
piensa usted necesitar alguna otra solicitud para un caso
especial, póngase en contacto con su oficina del INS que le
quede más cerca y pregúnteles. En ésta forma usted puede estar
absolútamente seguro de conseguir la solicitud correcta desde el
principio.

Adonde conseguir la solicitud

Se puede obtener una solicitud en persona o por correo de
su oficina del Servicio de Inmigración Y Naturalización más
cercana. Véase Apéndice 4, "Oficinas del INS en los E.U.A." y el
Apéndice 5, "Oficinas del INS de ultramar" para ver una lista
completa que incluye los números de teléfono. A veces, las
oficinas de Pasaportes que se encuentran en la oficina del
Secretario o Dependiente del Condado contienen una provisión de
solicitudes, pero debe de llamar primero para mayor seguridad.
Una ventaja que tiene el ir en persona es que puede recoger una
cópia de ése folleto útil de referencias, el Formulario N-17,
"Los Requerimientos de Naturalización e Informe General",
mientras que se encuentra usted ahi. Otra ventaja es que tambien
le pueden hacer su Carta de Huellas digitales, lo cual le ahorra
tiempo más adelante. Sin embargo, si le es más fácil escribir
pidiendo éstas cosas, solo puede copiar la carta que se le
demuestra en el ejemplar 5, pero tenga cuidado de usar la
dirección de la oficina del INS que le queda más cerca.

Cuando debe uno pedir la solicitud

Algunos inmigrantes pueden desear hacerse ciudadanos tan
pronto posible. Otros pueden vivir en los Estados Unidos por
años, y quizá, la mayoría de sus vidas antes de decidirse
hacerse ciudadanos. Mientras que nunca es demasiado tarde
comenzar el procedimiento de la solicitud, sí es posible
comenzarlo demasiado temprano. Tiene usted primero que llenar
el requisito de residencia por 5 años, o 3 anós si está casado
con ciudadano, antes de solicitar la naturalización. Otra vez,
puede desear usted consultar el Apéndice 1, "Las Excepciones de

Where To Get An Application

An application can be obtained in person or by mail from your nearest Immigration and Naturalization Service office. See Appendix 4, "INS Offices in the U.S.A." and Appendix 5, "INS Offices Overseas" for a complete listing including telephone numbers. Sometimes, Passport Offices located in your local County Clerk's office keep a supply of applications, but call first to make sure. An advantage to going personally is that you can pick up a copy of that handy reference pamphlet, Form N-17, "Naturalization Requirements and General Information," while you are there. Another advantage is that you can also get your fingerprint chart done, which saves time later on. However, if it is easier to write for these things, just copy the letter as shown in Sample 5, but be careful to use the address of the INS office closest to you.

When To Apply

Some immigrants may wish to become citizens at the earliest possible time. Others may live in the United States for years, maybe even most of their lives, before deciding to become citizens. While it is never too late to begin the application process, it is possible to begin too early. You must first meet the residency requirement of 5 years, or 3 years if married to a citizen, before applying for naturalization. Again, you may wish to refer to Appendix 1, "Exceptions to Residence & Physical Presence Requirements," for detailed information about the residency requirement and exceptions to it.

For extra efficiency, you can get an application just prior to meeting your residency requirement. This way, you can be completing the application during your final month or so, and it will be ready to mail or deliver immediately after your residency requirement has been met. Because the application is lengthy and takes considerable time to fill out, this is a good plan for those desiring to apply for citizenship at the earliest possible time. Bear in mind that once your application has been submitted, it can take a long time, probably more than a year, to be processed. So the sooner the Immigration and Naturalization Service office receives

Residencia y los Requisitos de Presencia Física", para encontrar un informe detallado sobre el requisito de residencia y las excepciones que le pertenecen.

Para mayor eficiencia, puede usted conseguir una solicitud inmediatamente antes de cumplir el requisito de la residencia. En ésta forma, puede usted estar teminando de llenar su solicitud durante el último mes, y ya estará listo para mandarlo por correo o entregarlo inmediatamente despues de que haya llenado su requisito de residencia. Ya que la solicitud es larga y toma bastante tiempo para llenarla, es buen plan para los que de sean solicitar la ciudadanía lo más pronto posible. Tenga en mente de que una vez que se entregue su solicitud, puede tardar mucho tiempo, probablemente más de un año, para que se tramita. Asi es que cuanto antes que pueda recibir su solicitud la oficina del Servicio de Inmigración y Naturalización que le queda más cerca, tendrá usted la preferencia de estar entre los más altos en la lista y asi puede tramitarse más pronto.

Como completar la solicitud

Las instrucciones se incluyen con el Formulario N-400, su "Solicitud para Iniciar la Petición de Naturalización". Véase el ejemplar 6, "Instrucciones para el Solicitante". Siga usted éstas instrucciones cuidadosamente y exactamente. Use una maquina de escribir si es posible, ó escribalo en tinta con letra de molde. Todos los artículos sobre la forma se deben de contestar a su mejor capacidad. Si alguna pregunta nó le es pertinente, no deje un espacio en blanco. Escriba, "not applicable", que quiere decir, no me es pertinente.

Puede ser que le ayude el que mire usted el ejemplar 1 cuando esté llenando su propia solicitud. Si alguna persona lo ayuda a llenarla, esté seguro que usted haya comprendido completamente cada pregunta y que la haya contestado con cuidado, totalmente y correctamente. Las preguntas y contestaciones de su solicitud serán una parte importante de su examen de naturalización por el cual determinará su escudriñador su maestría del inglés hablado.

your application, the higher up on the waiting list your application will be, and the sooner it can be processed.

How To Complete the Application

Instructions come with Form N-400, your "Application to File Petition for Naturalization." See Sample 6, "Instructions to the Applicant." Follow these instructions carefully and exactly. Use a typewriter if possible, or print neatly in ink. All items on the form should be answered to the best of your ability. If a question is not applicable, do not leave it blank. Write "not applicable."

It may be helpful for you to refer to Sample I while filling out your own application. If someone helps you fill it out, make sure that you completely understand every question and have answered carefully, fully, and accurately. The questions and answers on your application will be an important part of your naturalization examination whereby the examiner determines your mastery of spoken English.

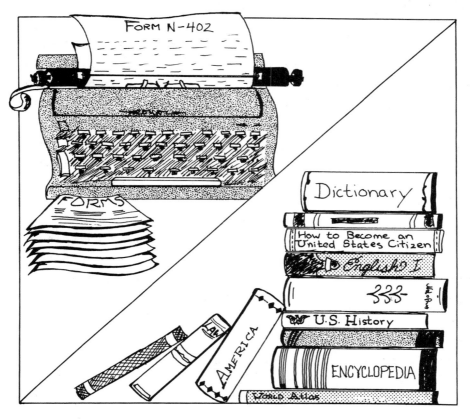

Sample 5
Sample letter to Obtain an Application

(Your street address)
(Your city, state, zip code)
(Today's date)

Immigration & Naturalization Service
(Street address)
(City, state, zip code)

Dear Sir:

I want to become a United States citizen.

Please mail to the above address Form N-17, "Naturalization Requirements and General Information" and also Form N-400, "Application to File Petition for Naturalization" with the fingerprint chart and "Biographic Information" sheet.

I look forward to receiving these things at your earliest convenience. Thank you.

Sincerely,
(Your Signature)

Example of a Fingerprint Card
(see Pages 48 & 49)

APPLICANT	LEAVE BLANK	TYPE OR PRINT ALL INFORMATION IN BLACK		FBI LEAVE BLANK

LAST NAME NAM   FIRST NAME   MIDDLE NAME

SIGNATURE OF PERSON FINGERPRINTED

ALIASES AKA

O
R
I

CAINSSFOO
USINS
SAN FRAN CA

RESIDENCE OF PERSON FINGERPRINTED

DATE OF BIRTH DOB
Month   Day   Year

CITIZENSHIP CTZ

| SEX | RACE | HGT. | WGT. | EYES | HAIR | PLACE OF BIRTH POB |

DATE   SIGNATURE OF OFFICIAL TAKING FINGERPRINTS

YOUR NO. OCA

LEAVE BLANK

EMPLOYER AND ADDRESS

FBI NO. FBI

CLASS _____

ARMED FORCES NO. MNU

REASON FINGERPRINTED

SOCIAL SECURITY NO. SOC

REF. _____

MISCELLANEOUS NO. MNU

1. R. THUMB	2. R. INDEX	3. R. MIDDLE	4. R. RING	5. R. LITTLE

6. L. THUMB	7. L. INDEX	8. L. MIDDLE	9. L. RING	10. L. LITTLE

LEFT FOUR FINGERS TAKEN SIMULTANEOUSLY   L. THUMB   R. THUMB   RIGHT FOUR FINGERS TAKEN SIMULTANEOUSLY

U.S. DEPARTMENT OF JUSTICE

IMMIGRATION AND NATURALIZATION SERVICE

APPLICATION TO FILE PETITION FOR NATURALIZATION

INSTRUCTIONS TO THE APPLICANT

(Tear off this instruction sheet before filling out this form)

You must be at least 18 years old to file a petition for naturalization. Using ink or a typewriter, answer every question in the application form, whether you are male or female. If you need more space for an answer, write "Continued" in your answer, then finish your answer on a sheet of paper this size, giving the number of the question.

YOU WILL BE EXAMINED UNDER OATH ON THE ANSWERS IN THIS APPLICATION WHEN YOU APPEAR FOR YOUR NATURALIZATION EXAMINATION.

If you wish to be called for examination at the same time as a relative who is applying for naturalization is called, attach a separate sheet so stating, and show the name and the Alien Registration Number of that relative.

1. **YOU MUST SEND WITH THIS APPLICATION THE FOLLOWING ITEMS (1), (2), (3) AND (4):**

(1) Photographs of your Face:

   a. Three identical unglazed copies, size 2 x 2 inches only.

   b. Taken within the last 30 days.

   c. Distance from top of head to point of chin to be 1¼ inches.

   d. On thin paper, with light background, showing front view without hat.

   e. In natural color or black and white, and not machine-made.

   f. Unsigned (but write Alien Registration Number lightly in pencil in center of reverse side).

(2) **Fingerprint Chart**—Complete all personal data items such as name, address, date of birth, sex, etc. Write your Alien Registration Number in the space marked "Your No. OCA" or "Miscellaneous No. MNU". You must sign the chart IN THE PRESENCE OF THE PERSON taking your fingerprints and have that person sign his/her name, title and date in the spaces provided. Take the chart and these instructions to a police station, sheriff's office, or an office of this Service, or other reputable person or organization for fingerprinting. (You should contact the police or sheriff's office first since some of these offices do not take fingerprints for other government agencies.) DO NOT BEND, FOLD OR CREASE THE FINGERPRINT CHART.

(3) **Biographic Information.**—Complete every item in the Biographic Information form furnished you with this application and sign your name on the line provided. If you have ever served in the Armed Forces of the United States, obtain and complete also an extra yellow sheet of the form, bearing the number G-325B.

(4) **U.S. Military Service.**—If your application is based on your military service, obtain and complete Form N—426, "Request for Certification of Military or Naval Service."

2. **FEE.**—DO NOT SEND any fee with this application unless you are also applying for a certificate of citizenship for a child (see Instruction 6).

3. **ALIEN REGISTRATION RECEIPT CARD.**—DO NOT SEND your Alien Registration Receipt Card with this application.

4. **EXAMINATION ON GOVERNMENT AND LITERACY.**—Every person applying for naturalization must show that he or she has a knowledge and understanding of the history, principles, and form of government of the United States. THERE IS NO EXEMPTION FROM THIS REQUIREMENT, and you will therefore be examined on these subjects when you appear before the examiner with your witnesses.

You will also be examined on your ability to read, write and speak English. If on the date of your examination you are more than 50 years of age and have been a lawful permanent resident of the United States for 20 or more years, you will be exempt from the English language requirements of the law. If you are exempt, you may take the examination in any language you wish.

5. **OATH OF ALLEGIANCE.**—You will be required to take the following oath of allegiance to the United States in order to become a citizen:

Form N-400 (Rev. 5-2-82) Y

(Over)

I hereby declare, on oath, that I absolutely and entirely renounce and abjure all allegiance and fidelity to any foreign prince, potentate, state or sovereignty, of whom or which I have heretofore been a subject or citizen; that I will support and defend the Constitution and laws of the United States of America against all enemies, foreign and domestic; that I will bear true faith and allegiance to the same; that I will bear arms on behalf of the United States when required by the law; that I will perform noncombatant service in the armed forces of the United States when required by the law; that I will perform work of national importance under civilian direction when required by the law; and that I take this obligation freely without any mental reservation or purpose of evasion; so help me God.

If you cannot promise to bear arms or perform noncombatant service because of religious training and belief, you may omit those promises when taking the oath.

"Religious training and belief" means a person's belief in a relation to a Supreme Being involving duties superior to those arising from any human relation, but does not include essentially political, sociological, or philosophical views or a merely personal moral code.

6. **THIS BLOCK APPLIES ONLY TO APPLICANTS WHO HAVE FOREIGN-BORN CHILDREN WHO ARE UNDER 18 YEARS OF AGE.**

Some or all of your *own* foreign-born children (Not Step-Children) who are not yet citizens may possibly become United States citizens automatically when you are naturalized. This will happen:

(1) If the child is a lawful permanent resident of the United States and still under 18 years of age when you are naturalized, and

(2) The child's other parent is already a citizen or becomes a citizen before or at the same time that you become naturalized. If, however, the child's other parent is deceased, or if you are divorced and have custody of the child, then it makes no difference that the child's other parent was or is an alien.

(3) If your child is illegitimate and you are the mother, only (1) above applies.

(4) If the child is adopted, and was adopted before its 16th birthday and is in your custody.

If you wish, you can apply for a Certificate of Citizenship for any of these children, which will show that they are United States citizens. If you do not want such a Certificate, write "DO NOT" in Question (36), page 3; if you do want such a Certificate, write "DO" in Question (36), page 3, and send the following with this application.

(1) Fee. Fifteen dollars ($15) for each child for whom a certificate is desired. DO NOT SEND CASH IN THE MAIL. ALL FEES MUST BE SUBMITTED IN THE EXACT AMOUNT. If you mail your application, attach a money order or check, payable to *Immigration and Naturalization Service*, (Exceptions: If you reside in the Virgin Islands, remittance must be payable to Commissioner of Finance, Virgin Islands; and if in Guam, to Treasurer, Guam). Personal checks are accepted subject to collectibility. An uncollectible check will render the application and any documents issued pursuant thereto invalid. A charge of $5.00 will be imposed if a check in payment of a fee is not honored by the bank on which it is drawn. The fee will be refunded if for any reason the child does not qualify for the certificate.

(2) **Personal Description Form.**—A completed Form N—604 for each child.

(3) **Documents.**—The documents applicable to your case listed in the blocks below. If you want any of the original documents returned to you, and if the law does not prohibit the making of copies, a photocopy of the document should be sent with the original document.

Any document in a foreign language must be accompanied by an English translation. The translation must contain a certification from the translator as to his competency as a translator and the accuracy of his translation.

(4) **Photographs.**—Follow Instruction No. one (1) and send three (3) photographs of each child. Write the child's Alien Registration Number on the back of the photographs, lightly in pencil.

DOCUMENTS REQUIRED WITH THIS APPLICATION

1. Child's birth certificate.
2. Your marriage certificate to child's other parent.
3. If you or the other parent were married before the marriage to each other, death certificate or divorce decree showing the termination of any previous marriage of each parent.
4. If the other parent became a citizen at birth, birth certificate of other parent.
5. If the child's other parent is deceased, or if you are divorced from the child's other parent, the death certificate or the divorce decree.
6. If the child is adopted, adoption decree.

SECONDARY EVIDENCE

If it is not possible to obtain any one of the required documents shown in the block above, consideration may be given to the following documents. In such case you must present a written explanation as to why the document listed in the block above is not being presented, together with a statement from the official custodian of the record showing that the document is not available.

1. *Baptismal certificate.*—A certificate under the seal of the church where the baptism occurred, showing date and place of child's birth, date of baptism, the names of the child's parents, and names of the godparents, if shown.

2. *School record.*—A letter from the school authorities having jurisdiction over the school attended (preferably the first school), showing date of admission to the school, child's date of birth or age at that time, place of birth, and the names and places of birth of parents, if shown in the school records.

3. If you or the other parent were married before the marriage to each other, death certificate or divorce decree showing the termination of any person(s) listed.

4. *Affidavits.*—Notarized affidavits of two persons who were living at the time, and who have personal knowledge of the event you are trying to prove—for example, the date and place of a birth, marriage, or death. The persons making the affidavits may be relatives and need not be citizens of the United States. Each affidavit should contain the following information regarding the person making the affidavit; His (Her) full name and address; date and place of birth; relationship to you, if any; full information concerning the event; and complete details concerning how he (she) acquired knowledge of the event.

Tres cosas merecen tener su atención especial cuando esté llenando su solicitud. Segun al menos uno de los oficiales de la inmgración, son cosas de las que los solicitantes se descuidan comunmente y las hacen incorrectamente.

1. **Conformidad**: Esté seguro de escribir su nombre exactamente igual en todas partes de la solicitud entera con excepción de la línea que dice "Otros nombres que he usado son ...".

2. **Arrestos**: Si le son pertinentes, llene el artículo 15 en la segunda página totalmente y correctamente. aunque sea por una violación del tránsito. Nó lo deje en blanco si alguna vez haya sido arrestado. Esto es súmamente importante, ya que una omisión aqui le puede poner en peligro a su naturalización. Séa usted totalmente honrado!

3. **Organizaciones**: El artículo 16 en la segunda página es importante. Su pertenecencia a clubs y a grupos pueden atestiguar de que esté usted capacitado para la ciudadanía. Nó le dé usted menosprecio ni deje de completar con cualesquiera que sea el grupo.

Aparte de la solicitud misma, necesitará completar la Carta de huellas digitales y tendrá que obtener fotos recientes conforme a las especificaciones que siguen:

La Carta De Huellas Digitales:

Antes de que escriba usted cualquier cosa sobre ésta tarjeta, dese cuenta que las instrucciones sobre su solicitud dicen que su firma se tendrá que dar en la presencia del oficial que le tóme sus huellas digitales. Nó firme la tarjeta al menos que el oficial tomando sus huellas digitales se lo indique.

Si recoge su solicitud en persona, el Formulario N-400, de una oficina del Servicio de Inmigración y Naturalización le pueden tomar ahi mismo y inmediatamente sus huellas digitales. Esta es la manera de hacerlo de mejor eficiencia. Es gratis y usted se ahorrará un viaje especial más tarde para solo tomar las huellas digitales. Pero si usted manda su solicitud por correo y la oficina del INS que le queda más cerca está bastante lejos, lláme a la oficina de su cerife o a la estación de la

Three items deserve your special attention when filling out your application. They are, according to at least one immigration official, items most commonly neglected or done incorrectly by applicants:

1. **Consistency:** Make sure your name is put down exactly the same throughout the entire application, except for the line that asks for other names you have used.

2. **Arrests:** If applicable, fill in item 15 on page 2 completely and accurately, even for a traffic violation. Do not leave it empty if you have **ever** been arrested. This is extremely important, as an ommission here could jeopardize your naturalization. Be completely honest!

3. **Organizations:** Item 16 on page 2 is important. Your membership in clubs and groups can help attest to your suitability for citizenship. Do not consider it unimportant and overlook any group.

Aside from the application itself, you will need to complete the fingerprint chart and get recent photographs to specifications as follows:

The Fingerprint Chart:

Before you write anything at all on the card, notice that the instructions on your application say that your signature must be given in the presence of the officer fingerprinting you. Do not sign the card until told to do so by the fingerprinting officer.

If you pick up your application, Form N-400, personally at an Immigration and Naturalization Service office, you can get your fingerprints done then and there. This is the most efficient way. It is free and will save you a special trip just for fingerprints later on. But if you sent for your application by mail, and your nearest INS office is quite far away, call your local sheriff's office or police station. State police generally provide better fingerprints than local police. When you call, ask them if they can take your fingerprints for your citizenship application, if there is any cost, and what time and on what days they do fingerprints.

policía. La policía del Estado generalmente hacen mejores Cartas de huellas digitales que la policía local. Cuando le llámen, pídales si le pueden tomar sus huellas digitales para su solicitud de ciudadanía y que si les cobrarán, y a que hora y en que día le pueden tomar sus huellas digitales.

Debe usted de llenar todo el informe de antecedentes personales sobre la tarjeta de las huellas digitales tal como se le explica en el artículo 2 de las "Instrucciones al Solicitante". Entonces cargue con su tarjeta y su hoja de instrucciones cuando vaya a que le tomen sus huellas digitales. Solo se puede usar la tarjeta que le provée el INS. Firme su nombre en frente del oficial. Y esté seguro de nó doblar, plegar o arrugar la Carta de huellas digitales.

Las buenas huellas digitales son importante! Un grupo mal hecho le puede retardar su solicitud. Asi es que verifique para estar seguro que la Carta de huellas digitales tiene:
* Las primeras dos conyunturas del dedo que aparece sobre la tarjeta, no solo la punta del dedo.
* Una cantidad adecuada de tinta ya que usando demasiada tinta causa manchas y demasiado poco no se alcanza a ver.
* Marcas limpias y claras, ya que marcas mal hechas probablemente nó se considerarán y en general, las rechazarán.
Además de conseguir un buen grupo de huellas digitales sobre su Carta, tambien necesitará las fotos exigidas.

Fotografías:
Primeramente, haga plan para que le tomen sus retratos dentro de los 30 días antes de entregar su solicitud. Cuando esté listo, se dará cuenta que los fotógrafos normalmente conocen bien las especificaciones de las 3 fotos. Sin embargo, para estar más seguro, cuando vaya con un fotógrafo, cargue con su hoja de "Instrucciones al Solicitante" para referirse al artículo 1, "Fotografías de su Cara". Algunos fotógrafos aceptan a cualquier momento que una persona llegue y le tienen sus fotos en minutos. Debe de llamar usted primero para ver si necesita una cita. Al recibir las 3 fotos, escriba inmediatamente su

You should fill out all the personal data information of the fingerprint chart as stated in item 2 of "Instructions to the Applicant." Then take both your card and your instruction sheet with you when you go to have your fingerprints taken. Only the card supplied by the INS may be used. Sign your name in front of the "officer." And be sure not to bend, fold, or crease the fingerprint chart.

Good fingerprints are important! A poor set could delay your application. So, check to make sure that your fingerprint chart has:
* The first two joints of the finger appearing on the card, not just the finger tip.
* The proper amount of ink, as too much ink causes smears. Too little ink cannot be deciphered.
* Neat and clear prints, as sloppy looking prints are probably bad prints and will generally be rejected.
In addition to getting a good set of fingerprints on your chart, you will also need the required photographs.

Photographs:
First of all, plan to have your pictures taken within the last 30 days prior to submitting your application. When you are ready, you will find that photographers are usually very familiar with the specifications for the 3 photos. However, just to be on the safe side when you go to the photographer, take with you your "Instructions to the Applicant" sheet for reference to item 1, "Photographs of your Face." Some photographers take walk-ins and have your pictures ready in minutes. You should call first to ask if you need an appointment. Upon receiving the 3 photos, immediately write your Alien Registration number and name on the back center of each one. Remember, once you have your photos, you have no more than 30 days in which to mail or personally deliver your entire, completed application to the Immigration and Naturalization Service office.

Submitting the Completed Application

Before you submit your completed application, whether in person or by mail, first tear off the "Instructions to the Applicant" sheet.

número de la "Mica" junto con su nombre en el doso y en el centro de cada una. Recuérdese que una vez que haya tomado sus fotos, tiene usted no más de 30 dias para mandarlas por correo o para entregarlas en persona junto con su solicitud entera que haya completado a la oficina del Servicio de Inmigración y Naturalización.

Entregando la solicitud

Antes de entregar su solicitud terminada, sea en persona o por correo, primero arranque la hoja de "Instrucciones al Solicitante". Luego junte todas las partes de su solicitud. Suponiendo que usó usted el N-400, entonces debe de tener:

1. La Solicitud para Iniciar la Petición de Naturalización, Formulario N-400
2. La Hoja de Informe Biográfico, G-325.
3. La Carta de Huellas Digitales.
4. Las tres fotografías.
5. Cualquier documentación que debe de acompañarlos.

No mande dinero con su solicitud, al menos que incluya a sus hijos y en ése caso debe de incluir $15.00 por cada hijo por el cual desea usted tener un Certificado de Ciudadanía.

Antes de que salga de sus manos su solicitud, haga fotoscópia de todo. En ésta forma tendrá usted el duplicado para usarlo como referencia al preparar su examen preliminar, el cual es el segundo paso del procedimiento de naturalización. Tambien, al guardarse usted su cópia, tendrá algo de referencia si a caso se le pierde la solicitud que entregó.

Si manda por correo su solicitud, use un sobre grande, preferiblemente uno que mida 9 por 12 pulgadas. Escriba la dirección de la oficina del INS que le queda más cerca y ponga su propia dirección en la esquina alta del lado izquierdo del sobre. Haga que el dependiente postal le pese su sobre para determinar la cantidad exacta que necesita de porte. Debido a la importancia del contenido, puede decidir usted mandarlo por "correo certificado con acuso de recibo". En ésta forma tiene usted una verificación que el INS recibió su solicitud. Una ves

Next, assemble all the parts of your application together. Assuming you used N-400, you should have:

1. The Application to File Petition for Naturalization, Form N-400.
2. The Biographic Information Sheet, G-325.
3. The Fingerprint Chart.
4. The 3 Photographs.
5. Any required accompanying documents.

Do not send any money with your application, unless it includes children, in which case you enclose $15.00 for each child for whom you would like a Certificate of Citizenship.

Before your application leaves your hands, make a photocopy of everything. This way you will have it for reference in preparation for your preliminary examination, which is step two in the process of naturalization. Also, by keeping a copy for yourself you will have something to refer to in case the application you submitted is lost.

If you mail your application in, use a large envelope, preferably a size 9 x 12 inches. Address it to your nearest INS office and put your return address in the upper left corner of the envelope. Have the postal clerk weigh your envelope to determine the exact amount of postage. Because of the importance of the contents, you may decide to send it by "certified" mail with a return receipt. This way, you have verification that the INS did receive your application. Once the application is out of your hands, there comes a long, long wait.

Your waiting time can be put to good use. Use it to learn the basic facts about United States history and government. This knowledge is required in order for you to pass the preliminary examination, the next big step on the way to becoming a United States citizen.

que su solicitud esté fuera de sus manos, entonces le viene una
espera muy, muy larga.

Puede usted utilizar bien su tiempo de espera. Úselo para
conocer los hechos de la historia y el gobierno de los Estados
Unidos. Este conocimiento se le exige para que usted pueda pasar
su examen preliminar, que es el siguiente paso grande camino al
que se vuelva usted ciudadano de los Estados Unidos.

Capitulo 3
EL EXAMEN PRELIMINAR

Despues de entregar su solicitud terminada, sea por correo o en persona al Servicio de Inmigración y Naturalización, puede usted contar con una espera larga de al menos varios meses antes de que le notifiquen cuando y adonde debe de comparecer para su examen preliminar. Cada persona que solicita su naturalización sin excepción, tiene que tomar éste examen, el cual forma el segundo paso, camino a su ciudadanía.

La Naturaleza del examen

Un escrudiñador de naturalización le hará preguntas sobre su solicitud, el Formulario N-400 para estar seguro de que esté completo y en la debida orden para registrarlo con la corte. Le harán preguntas bajo juramento y el escrudiñador estará seguro que usted:

1. Reúna los requisitos de residencia y de presencia física,
2. de que sea usted una persona honrada,
3. de que nó tenga alguna conexión con ninguna organización subversiva,
4. de que tenga conocimiento de la historia y el gobierno de los Estados, y
5. de que pueda leer, escribir y hablar el inglés.

El escrudiñador de naturalización le hace las preguntas verbalmente en un inglés sencillo. Una razón principal para el capítulo 3 de éste libro es el ayudarle a aprender suficientemente de la historia y el gobierno de los Estados Unidos para que pueda tomar y terminar éste examen. Hay 102 preguntas y contestaciones aqui abajo que cubren el conocimiento necesario.

Si le parece que ud reúne los requisitos para naturalizarse, entonces el escrudiñador le pedirá que firme su solicitud, el Formulario N-400 en la sección que dice, "Nó llene ningun blanco debajo de ésta Línea". Entonces se le entrega al secretario de la corte y él llena una planilla formal "La Petición para Naturalización", el Formulario N-405, tal como se ve en el ejemplar no. 7. Usted va a leer ésta petición

Chapter 3
THE PRELIMINARY EXAMINATION

After submitting your completed application by mail or in person to the Immigration and Naturalization Service, expect a long wait of at least several months before being notified when and where to appear for the preliminary examination. Every person applying for naturalization, with no exceptions, must take this examination, which is step two on the way to citizenship.

The Nature Of the Examination

A naturalization examiner will question you about your application, Form N-400, to make sure that it is complete and in proper order for filing with the court. You will be questioned under oath by an examiner in order to make certain that you:
1. meet the residency and physical presence requirements,
2. are of good moral character,
3. have no connection with any subversive organization,
4. have a knowledge of United States history and government, and
5. are able to read, write and speak English.
The questions are given orally, in simple English, by the naturalization examiner. One main goal of Chapter 3 of this book is to help you to learn enough about United States history and government so you can get through this examination. There are 102 questions and answers below which cover the necessary knowledge.

If it appears that you meet the requirements for naturalization, the examiner will ask you to sign your application, Form N-400, under the section, "Do Not Fill in Blanks Below This Line." It is then given to the clerk of the court who fills out a formal "Petition for Naturalization," Form N-405, as shown in Sample 7. You will read this petition carefully, then sign and swear to it. At this time, you must pay to the clerk of the naturalization court a $50.00 fee for filing your petition. Active duty members of the United States

Sample 7 - Form N-405
Petition for Naturalization

PETITION FOR NATURALIZATION

U.S. DEPARTMENT OF JUSTICE
IMMIGRATION AND NATURALIZATION SERVICE

PETITION FOR NATURALIZATION

ORIGINAL
(To be retained
by Clerk of Court)

Petition No. __947785__

A.R. No. __A 55 416 038__

To the Honorable __Naturalization__ Court for the __U.S. District__ at __Los Angeles__

This petition for naturalization, hereby made and filed under section __316 (a)__,
Immigration and Nationality Act, respectfully shows:

(1) My full, true, and correct name is __Pedro Garcia-Gonzalez__
(Full, true name, without abbreviations)

(2) My present place of residence is __621 E. Emmett St.__ __Santa Ana,__
(Apt. No.) (Number and street) (City or town)
__Orange__ __California__ __92707__
(County) (State) (Zip Code)

(3) I was born on __Dec. 3, 1940__, in __San Pulco, Zacatecas, Mexico__

(4) I request that my name be changed to __Pete Garcia__

(5) I was lawfully admitted to the United States for permanent residence and have not abandoned such residence.

(6) (If petition filed under Section 316(a).) I have resided continuously in the United States for at least five years and continuously in the State in which this petition is made for at least six months, immediately preceding the date of this petition and after my lawful admission for permanent residence, and I have been physically present in the United States for at least one-half of such five year period.

(7) (If petition filed under Section 319(a).) I have resided continuously in the United States in marital union with my present spouse for at least three years immediately preceding the date of this petition, and after my lawful admission for permanent residence, during all of which period my said spouse has been a United States citizen, and have been physically present in the United States at least one-half of such three-year period. I have resided continuously in the State in which this petition is made at least six months immediately preceding the date of this petition.

(8) (If petition is filed under Section 319 (b).) My present spouse is a citizen of the United States, in the employment of the Government of the United States, or of an American institution of research recognized as such by the Attorney General, or an American firm or corporation engaged in whole or in part in the development of foreign trade and commerce of the United States, or subsidiary thereof, or of a public international organization in which the United States participates by treaty or statute, or is authorized to perform the ministerial or priestly functions of a religious denomination having a bona fide organization within the United States, or is engaged solely as a missionary by a religious denomination or by an interdenominational mission organization having a bona fide organization within the United States, and such spouse is regularly stationed abroad in such employment. I intend in good faith upon naturalization to live abroad with my spouse and to resume my residence within the United States immediately upon termination of such employment abroad.

(9) (If petition is filed under Section 328.) I have served honorably in the Armed Forces of the United States for a period or periods aggregating three years. I have never been separated from the Armed Forces of the United States under other than honorable conditions. If not still in service, my service terminated within six months of the filing of my petition.

(10) (If petition is filed under Section 329.) While an alien or noncitizen national of the United States, I served honorably in an active-duty status in the military, air, or naval forces of the United States during either World War I or during a period beginning September 1, 1939, and ending December 31, 1946, or during a period beginning June 25, 1950, and ending July 1, 1955, or during a period beginning February 28, 1961, and ending October 15, 1978, or I was discharged after five years of service under the Act of June 30, 1950 (P.L. 597, 81st Congress). If separated from such service, I was separated under honorable conditions. At the time of enlistment, reenlistment, or induction I was in the United States, the Canal Zone, American Samoa, or Swains Island. If not in any of these places, I was lawfully admitted to the United States for permanent residence subsequent to enlistment or induction. I was never separated from such service on account of alienage. I was not a conscientious objector who performed no military, air, or naval duty whatever or refused to wear the uniform. I have not previously been naturalized on the basis of the same period of service.

(11) I am not and have not been, within the meaning of the Immigration and Nationality Act, for a period of at least 10 years immediately preceding the date of this petition, a member of or affiliated with any organization proscribed by such Act, or any section, subsidiary, branch, affiliate or subdivision thereof, nor have I during such period believed in, advocated, engaged in, or performed any of the acts or activities prohibited by such Act.

(12) I am, and have been during all the periods required by law, a person of good moral character, attached to the principles of the Constitution of the United States and well disposed to the good order and happiness of the United States.

(13) It is my intention in good faith to become a citizen of the United States and take without qualification the oath of renunciation and allegiance prescribed by the Immigration and Nationality Act, and to reside permanently in the United States. I am willing, when required by law, to bear arms on behalf of the United States, to perform noncombatant service in the Armed Forces of the United States, and to perform work of national importance under civilian director (unless exempted therefrom).

(14) I am able to read, write, and speak the English language (unless exempted therefrom), and I have a knowledge and understanding of the fundamentals of the history, and of the principles and form of government of the United States.

(15) Wherefore I request that I may be admitted a citizen of the United States of America. I swear (affirm) that I know the contents of this petition for naturalization subscribed by me, and that the same are true to the best of my knowledge and belief, and that this petition is signed by me with my full, true name. So Help Me God.

(16)

Pedro Garcia-Gonzalez
(Full Name, Without Abbreviations)

WHEN OATH ADMINISTERED BY CLERK OR DEPUTY CLERK OF COURT	WHEN OATH ADMINISTERED BY DESIGNATED EXAMINER
Subscribed and sworn to (affirmed) before me by above-named petitioner in the respective forms of oath shown in said petition and affidavit, and filed by said petitioner, in the office of the clerk of said court at _____ this _____ day of _____, 19 _____	Subscribed and sworn to (affirmed) before me by above-named petitioner in the respective forms of oath shown in said petition and affidavit at _____ this _____ day of _____, 19 _____
_____ Clerk.	_____ Designated Examiner.
_____ Deputy Clerk.	I HEREBY CERTIFY that the foregoing petition for naturalization was by petitioner named herein filed in the office of the clerk of said court at _____ this _____ day of _____, 19 _____
[SEAL]	_____ Clerk.
	_____ Deputy Clerk.

FORM N—405 (REV. 4-1-82)N

Presidents of the United States

cuidadosamente, entonces la firmará y tomará juramento del mismo. En éste entoces usted tendrá que pagarle al secretario de la corte de naturalización un honorario de $50.00 para que registren su petición. Nó se les exige pago a los miembros de las fuerzas armadas de los Estados Unidos en Facción activo. Este es el único honorario que se exige para su naturalización.

Se les pide a los hijos que automaticamente se vuelven ciudadanos a través de la naturalización de sus padres y que tengan los años necesarios para poder firmar un Certificado de Ciudadanía que estén presentes para el examen de sus padres. Sin embargo no se les exige pasar el examen de inglés o los requisitos de naturalización (se encuentran en el Capítulo 1).

Si usted nó reune todos los requisitos para la naturalización, el escrudiñador le dirá y, probablemente le recomendará que tome alguna acción para corregirlo. Por ejemplo, si su conocimiento del inglés o de la historia y el gobierno de los Estados Unidos no es bastante bueno, el escrudiñador le puede sugerir que se le registra su petición de todas formas, pero que se le postergue su examen para una fecha en el futuro cuando esté usted mejor preparado. Si hay alguna deficiencia grave, el escrudiñador le puede aconsejar que nó registre usted la petición.

Ya Nó Se Necesitan Testigos Para El Examen:

Recienmente ha habido un cambio mayor tocante a los testigos. Un solicitante para naturalización ya no se le requiere que traiga a dos ciudadanos de los Estados Unidos como testigos al examen. El requerimiento del testigo a la reputación de una persona se ha eliminado con una modernización de las leyes de Inmigración de los Estados Unidos que se firmó por el Presidente Reagan como ley el 29 de diciembre de 1981.

Los Requisitos Escolares Para Pasar El Examen:

Se le exige a un solicitante que tenga conocimiento del inglés, que pueda escribir y leerlo sencillamente y que tenga conocimiento de la historia y gobierno de los Estados Unidos. Hay ciertas excepciones a éstos requisitos, los cuales se explican en el Apéndice 6, "Informe Referente a la Escuela sobre la Ciudadanía para llenar los Requisitos de Naturalización".

armed forces do not have to pay. This is the only fee required for your naturalization.

Children who automatically become citizens through their parents' naturalization and who are old enough to sign a Certificate of Citizenship are requested to attend their parents' examination. However, they are not required to pass the English test or the citizenship requirements of naturalization (listed in Chapter 1). Children under age 14 do not have to take the Oath of Allegiance.

If you do not meet all the requirements for naturalization, the examiner will tell you and probably recommend corrective action. For example, if your knowledge of English or United States history and government is not good enough, the examiner may suggest that your petition be filed anyway, but that the examination be postponed until a later date when you are better prepared. If there is a serious deficiency, the examiner may advise you not to file the petition.

Witnesses No Longer Required for the Examination:
A major change has recently taken place regarding witnesses. An applicant for naturalization is no longer required to bring along two United States citizens as witnesses to the examination. This character witness requirement has been eliminated by an update of the Immigration Laws of the United States which President Reagan signed into law on December 29, 1981.

Educational Requirements to Pass the Examination:
An applicant is required to have a knowledge of English, simple writing and reading skills, and a knowledge of United States history and government. There are certain exceptions to the requirements, which are explained in Appendix 6, "Information Concerning Citizenship Education to Meet Naturalization Requirements."

Lack of knowledge of spoken English is often the biggest stumbling block in meeting the educational requirements for prospective citizens. In fact, much of the examination is designed to test your knowledge of simple English. An applicant may be asked

La falta del conocimiento del inglés hablado, muy seguidamente es un tropezadero para llenar los requisitos educacionales de los ciudadanos anticipados. Verdaderamente, mucho del examen está diseñado para examinar el conocimiento del inglés sencillo. A un solicitante se le puede preguntar unas pocas preguntas sobre la historia y el gobierno, y ésto en general toma solo una porción pequeña del tiempo para el examen preliminar. Se le pedirá tambien que léa y escríba unas pocas frases o expresiones en inglés. La mayoría de la entrevista probablemente tendrá que ver con las preguntas sobre su solicitud. Normalmente las preguntas que le hacen son pocas y sencillas. Si el escrudiñador tiene alguna duda de su conocimiento y comprensión de la historia y el gobierno de los Estados Unidos, entonces puede prolongar las preguntas.

Su maestría del inglés hablado es de suma importancia! Los reglamentos dicen que "la capacidad del peticionario para hablar el inglés se determinará por las contestaciones y las preguntas que se hacen normalmente durante el curso de la entrevista preliminar" o el examen. Asi es que para poder llenar el requisito educacional, esté completamente familiarizado con las preguntas y las contestaciones en el Formulario N-400 y el Formulario N-325 tambien. Ésta es la razón que le servirá de mucho la fotoscópia que tomó de su solicitud antes de entregarla, como un estudio.

Además del requisito del idoma inglés, debe de tener un conocimiento básico de la historia y el gobierno de los E.U. Puede usted aprenderlo en casa al familiarizarse con las 102 preguntas y contestaciones aqui abajo. Pruebe diferentes tácticas cuando las estudie. Primero, solo léa un grupo pequeño, como quizas 3 o 5 preguntas y contestaciones, una y dos veces; segundo, léa solo las preguntas, cubriendo las contestaciones. Véa cuanto alcanza a recordar. ¿Se le olvidó una? Mire otra vez la contestación. Repase el grupo por la tercera vez, pero ésta vez, escriba cualquier contestación que nó pudo contestar. Estudie solo ésas contestaciones. A la cuarta vez, le saldrán probablemente todas bien y estará listo para seguir adelante con el grupo de 3 o 5 preguntas y contestaciones que siguen, repitiendo el proceso.

only a few questions on history and government, and this generally takes just a small portion of the time at the preliminary hearing. You will also be asked to read or write a few sentences or expressions in English. Most of the interview will probably be concerned with questions on your application. Ordinarily, the questions asked are few and simple. If the examiner has some doubt about your knowledge and understanding of United States history and government, the questioning could be prolonged.

Your mastery of spoken English is of vital importance! The regulations state that "the ability of a petitioner to speak English shall be determined from answers to questions normally asked in the course of the preliminary interview," or examination. Therefore, in order to meet the educational requirement, be thoroughly familiar with the questions and your answers on Form N-400 and Form N-325, too. This is why the photocopy you made of your application before submitting it will come in very handy for study purposes.

In addition to the English language requirement, you must have a basic knowledge of U.S. history and government. "Government" means, for the most part, the Constitution. You can accomplish this right at home by familiarizing yourself with the 102 questions and answers below. Try various techniques when you study them. First, just read through a small group, like maybe 3 or 5 questions and answers, once or twice. Second, read just the questions, with the answers covered up. See how much you remember. Forget one? Look at the answer again. Go through the group a third time, but this time write down any answer you missed. Study only those answers. By the fourth try, you will probably get them all right and be ready to take on the next group of 3 or 5 questions and answers, repeating the procedure.

Remember, you will most likely have many months to study from the time you submit your application Form N-400 until the time of your preliminary examination. This allows ample time to study about United States history and government in preparation for the preliminary examination. Read through the Constitution of the United States of America at least once. It appears in Appendix 7. It is truly a fascinating document which will not only add to your knowledge and understanding but also add to your appreciation of United States government.

Acuérdese, probablemente tendrá muchos meses para estudiar, comenzando desde el tiempo que entregó usted su solicitud, el Formulario N-400 hasta el tiempo de su examen preliminar. Esto le permite suficiente tiempo para estudiar sobre la historia y el gobierno de los Estados Unidos y prepararse para tomar su examen preliminar. Léa toda la Constitución de los Estados Unidos al menos una vez. Aparece en el Apéndice 7. Es un documento verdaderamente fascinante que no solo le incrementará su conocimiento y su comprensión pero tambien su aprecio por el gobierno de los Estados Unidos.

Lea la Constitución, estudie las 102 preguntas y contestaciones. Esto lo prepara para la porción del examen que se trata de la historia y el gobierno de los Estados Unidos. Entonces, cuando reciba la notificación de que se presente para su audiencia preliminar, la cual incluye el examen, póngase a repasar otra vez las 102 preguntas y contestaciones. Una buena manera de hacerlo es de pedirle a otra persona que le haga las preguntas en cualquier orden, y entonces dé usted las contestaciones. Haga que ésta persona le tome dato de cualquier pregunta que nó pudo contestar. Concéntrese en éstas antes de ir a tomar su examen. Si usted estudia seriamente éstas preguntas y contestaciones, no tendrá ninguna razón por la cual temer. Vuelva a leer la Constitución y revise cuidadosamente su N-400, y estará usted listo!

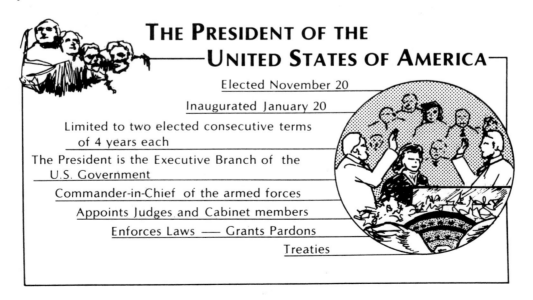

THE PRESIDENT OF THE
UNITED STATES OF AMERICA

Elected November 20

Inaugurated January 20

Limited to two elected consecutive terms of 4 years each

The President is the Executive Branch of the U.S. Government

Commander-in-Chief of the armed forces

Appoints Judges and Cabinet members

Enforces Laws —— Grants Pardons

Treaties

Read the Constitution, study the 102 questions and answers. This will prepare you for the United States history and government portion of the examination. Then, when you receive notification to appear for your preliminary hearing, which includes the examination, very carefully review the 102 questions and answers again. A good way to do this is to have another person ask you the questions, in any order, and **you** give the answers. Have that person keep a record of which questions you missed. Focus on those before going in for the examination. If you seriously study these questions and answers, you have no reason to be fearful. Re-read the Constitution and carefully look over your N-400, and you will be ready!

GROWTH OF THE CONSTITUTION

Introduced By . . .

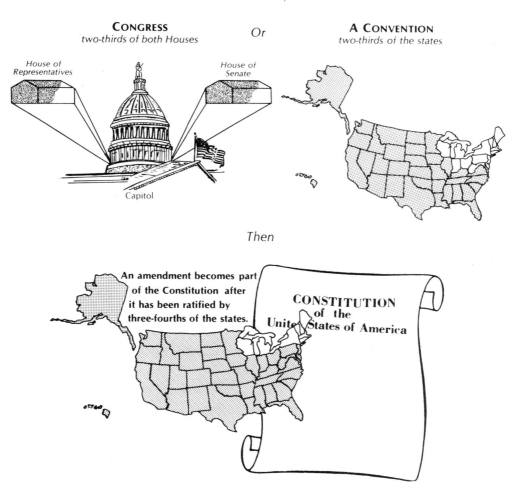

CONGRESS
two-thirds of both Houses

Or

A CONVENTION
two-thirds of the states

House of Representatives

House of Senate

Capitol

Then

An amendment becomes part of the Constitution after it has been ratified by three-fourths of the states.

CONSTITUTION
of the
United States of America

102 preguntas y contestaciones sobre la Historia de los E.U. y su Gobierno

Nota: En muchos casos, las contestaciones que se dan parecen ser incompletas o incorrectas. Sin embargo, no importa lo que piense usted de ellas, éstas son las contestaciones que espera oír el INS.

América, El Mundo Nuevo

1. ¿Cuando se descubrió la América y por quien?

    En 1492, un Italiano llamado Cristobal Colón pensó incorrectamente que había llegado a la India pero en realidad, descubrio el "Nuevo Mundo", la América.

2. ¿Por que han venido a vivir a los Estados Unidos las gentes de todas partes del mundo?

    Han venido por muchas razones, pero principalmente para compartir totalmente de las libertades que les ofrece los E.U. a sus ciudadanos.

3. ¿Adonde se estableció la primera instalación inglesa en la América?

    Se fundó en Jamestown, Virginia en el año 1607.

4. ¿Cuantas colonias primero formaron los E.U.? Cuantas puede usted nombrar?

    En 1776, habían 13 colonias de la Gran Bretaña: Connecticut, Delaware, Georgia, Maryland, Massachusetts, New Hampshire, New York, North Carolina, Pennsylvania, Rhode Island, South Carolina y Virginia. Estas colonias se unieron y formaron los primeros Estados Unidos.

5. ¿Cual fué la causa principal del pleito entre las colonias y su patria, la Gran Bretaña?

    La Imposición de impuestos sin representación. Los colonos creían que era una gran injusticia forzarlos a pagar impuestos cuando nó tenían representación en el Parlamento Británico.

6. ¿Qué fué la Fiesta de Té de Boston?

    El Rey y el Parlamento al fin se pusieron de acuerdo para revocar todos los impuestos con excepción del que llevaba

102 Questions and Answers
On U.S. History and Government

Note: In many cases, the answers given may seem incomplete or even inaccurate. However, whatever you may think of them, these are the answers expected by the INS.

America, The New World

1. When was America discovered and by whom?

    In 1492, an Italian by the name of Christopher Columbus mistakenly thought he had reached India but had in fact discovered the "New World," America.

2. Why have people from all over the world come to the United States to live?

    They have come for many reasons, but mainly to fully share in the freedoms the United States offers to its citizens.

3. Where was the first successful English settlement in America?

    It was founded in Jamestown, Virginia, in the year 1607.

4. How many colonies first made up the United States? How many can you name?

    In 1776, there were 13 British colonies: Connecticut, Delaware, Georgia, Maryland, Massachusetts, New Hampshire, New Jersey, New York, North Carolina, Pennsylvania, Rhode Island, South Carolina, and Virginia. These colonies joined together and became the first United States.

5. What was the main cause of dispute between the colonies and their "mother country," Great Britain?

    Taxation without representation. The colonists believed that it was especially unfair to force them to pay taxes when they had no representation in the British Parliament.

6. What was the Boston Tea Party?

    The King and Parliament finally agreed to repeal all of the taxes, except the one on tea. Then in 1773, The British East India Company shipped millions of pounds of tea to the colonists. The colonists would not permit the tea to be removed from the ships. Several ships returned to Great

el té. Entonces, en 1773, la Compañía Británica de la India del Oriente mandó por barco millones de libras de té para los colonos. Los colonos nó permitían que se removiera el té de los barcos y tiraron el té al mar en el Puerto.

7. ¿Qué es la Declaración de Independencia?

Este documento famoso le anunció al mundo la separación y la independencia de las 13 colonias de la Gran Bretaña. Estas colonias primero se hicieron los 13 Estados y luego nacieron como los Estados Unidos de América.

8. ¿Quién escribió la Declaración de Independencia?

Tomás Jefferson, un miembro y líder del comité nombrado por el Segundo Congreso Continental para escribir la mayoría del Escrito.

9. ¿Cuando celebramos el cumpleaños de la nación?

El 4 de julio de 1776 marca el nacimiento de los Estados Unidos de América. El Cuatro de Julio, conocido como el Diá de la Independencia es una fiesta nacional y las gentes en los Estados Unidos celebran éste día

10. ¿Cuando y adonde se firmó la Declaración de Independencia?

El 4 de julio de 1776 fué aceptada por el Segundo Congreso Continental en Filadelfia pero nó todos los delegados la firmaron hasta casi un mes después.

11. ¿Qué fué la Guerra de la Revolución?

El Rey Jorge estaba enojado por la declaración de Independencia y decidió que la Gran Bretaña iba a pelear para retener las colonias. Mientras tanto, el Rey tenía dificultades en casa. La Gran Bretaña se encontraba en una guerra con España y Francia. En éste tiempo, la Francia mandó ayuda a las colonias. La Guerra de la Revolución fué una guerra larga y dura que terminó con la entrega de vencimiento por el comandante Británico, Lord Cornwallis. Sin embargo, no fué hasta dos años despues, en 1783 que se firmó un trato de paz entre la Gran Bretaña y los nuevos Estados Unidos. Con éste trato, la Gran Bretaña reconoció a los Estados Unidos como nación independiente.

12. ¿Qué fueron los Artículos de la Confederación?

Los Artículos de la Confederación fue un documento y la primera prueba por las 13 colonias para establecer un dominio. Ya que los Artículos no le dieron suficiente

Britain. In Boston, Massachusetts, the colonists boarded the ships and threw the tea in the harbor.

7. What is the Declaration of Independence?

This famous document announced to the world the separation and independence of the 13 colonies from Great Britain. Those colonies became the first 13 states, and the United States of America was born.

8. Who wrote most of the Declaration of Independence?

Thomas Jefferson, a leading member of a committee appointed by the Second Continental Congress, did most of the writing.

9. When do we celebrate our nation's birthday?

July 4, 1776, marks the birth of the United States of America. The Fourth of July, known as Independence Day, is a national holiday, and people in the United States celebrate this day.

10. When and where was the Declaration of Independence signed?

On July 4, 1776, it was accepted by the Second Continental Congress in Philadelphia, but it was not signed by all delegates until almost a month later.

11. What was the Revolutionary War?

King George was angered by the Declaration of Independence and decided that Great Britain would fight to keep the colonies. Meanwhile, the King had trouble at home, as Great

poder al gobierno central para poder parar las riñas entre los estados, se descartó y con ésto se abrió el camino para que se escribiera la Constitución de los Estados Unidos.

13. ¿Cuantos estados existen en los Estados Unidos y cual es la capital?

Hay 50 estados, Washington, D.C. (Distrito de Colómbia), que nó es un estado, es la capital.

14. ¿Cuales son los territorios de los Estados Unidos?

Puerto Rico, las Islas Vígenes, Samoa y las Islas de Guam son territorios de los Estados Unidos. No se han ratificado como nuevos estados.

15. ¿Cuan grande son los Estados Unidos continentales?

Abarcan aproximadamente 2500 millas de la costa del Atlántico a la costa del Pacífico y aproximadamente 1300 millas del Canada a México.

El Gobierno De Los E.U.A.

16. ¿Qué forma de gobierno tienen los Estados Unidos?

El gobierno es una república, una república demócrata, que la definó Abraham Lincoln como "un gobierno del pueblo, por el pueblo y para el pueblo".

17. ¿Cuales son los 3 niveles de gobierno en los E.U.A.?

Son el federal, el estatal y el local.

18. ¿Qué es la Constitución?

Es la "ley suprema de la tierra". La Constitución defina la construcción y los poderes del gobierno federal. Las leyes estatales y locales nó pueden estar en conflicto con la Constitución.

19. ¿Cuando comenzó su vigencia la Constitución?

Comenzó a funcionar bajo la Constitución en 1778.

20. ¿Puede cambiarse la Constitución?

Si, se pueden hacer cambios con adiciones que se llaman "enmiendas".

21. ¿Qué es el "Bill of Rights"(La Carta de Derechos)?

Son las primeras 10 enmiendas de la Constitución. Todas las 10 se ratificaron (aprobaron) como un grupo en 1791.

Britain was at war with Spain and France. At this time France sent help to the colonies. The Revolutionary War was a long and hard war which ended with the surrender of the British commander, Lord Cornwalis. However, it was not until two years later, in 1783, that a peace treaty was signed between Great Britain and the new United States. By this treaty, Britain recognized the United States as an independent nation.

12. What were the Articles of Confederation?

The Articles of Confederation were the first attempt by the 13 colonies to set up self-government. Since the Articles did not give enough power to the central government to stop the quarreling among the states, they were discarded, and that paved the way for the writing of the Constitution of the United States.

13. How many states are there in the United States, and where is the capital?

There are 50 states. Washington, D.C. (District of Columbia), which is **not** a state, is the capital.

14. What are the territories of the United States?

Puerto Rico, the Virgin Islands, Samoa, and the Guam Islands are territories of the United States. They have not been ratified as new states.

15. How big is the continental United States?

It is approximately 2500 miles from the Atlantic coast to the Pacific coast and about 1300 miles from Canada to Mexico.

The Government of the U.S.A.

16. What is the form of government of the United States?

The government is a republic, or democratic republic, which was defined by Abraham Lincoln as "a government of the people, by the people, and for the people."

17. What are the 3 levels of government in the U.S.A.?

They are federal, state and local.

18. What is the Constitution?

It is the "supreme law of the land." The Constitution defines the construction and the powers of the federal government. State and local laws must not conflict with the Constitution.

22. ¿Cuales son algunos de los muy importante derechos garantizados por el "Bill of Rights:?

Entre otras cosas, el "Bill of Rights" protege la libertad de hablar, la libertad de la prensa, la libertad de la religión, el derecho de asambléo pacífico, y el derecho a un juicio justo.

23. ¿Cuantas enmiendas tiene la Constitución?

Al tiempo presente tiene 26. Desde las primeras 10 que forman el "Bill of Rights", han habido solo 16 más enmiendas añadidas desde 1791.

24. ¿Cuales son algunas de las más Importantes enmiendas del Bill of Rights?

No. 13   La revocación de la esclavitud

No. 19   Darles a las mujeres el derecho de votar

No. 22   Limitar al Presidente a dos términos de 4 años en su puesto.

No. 26   Bajar la edad mínima para votar a 18 años.

19. When did the Constitution take effect?

    The United States began to function under the Constitution in 1789.

20. Can the Constitution be changed?

    Yes, changes can be made by additions called "amendments."

21. What is the Bill of Rights?

    It is the first 10 amendments to the Constitution. All 10 were ratified (approved) as a group in 1791.

22. What are some very important rights guaranteed by the Bill of Rights?

    Among other things, the Bill of Rights protects our freedom of speech, freedom of the press, freedom of religion, the right to peaceably assemble, and the right to a fair trial.

23. How many amendments has the Constitution?

    There are 26 at present. Since the first 10, the Bill of Rights, there have been only 16 more amendments added since 1791.

24. What are some of the most important amendments after the Bill of Rights?

    No. 13   Abolished slavery
    No. 19   Gave women the right to vote
    No. 22   Limited the President to two 4-year terms in office
    No. 26   Lowered the minimum voting age to 18 years old

25. ¿Como se puede enmendar la Constitución?

Las enmiendas pueden ser propuestas por dos terceras partes del voto de las Casas del Congreso o por una convención nacional llamada por el Congreso por petición de dos terceras partes del cuerpo legislativo estatal. Para volverse ley, las enmiendas entonces deben de ser ratificadas (aprobadas) por el cuerpo legislativo de tres cuartas partes de los estados.

26. ¿Cuantos años debe de tener un ciudadano para votar?

Un ciudadano debe de tener al menos 18 años segun la Enmienda 26 (1971). Otro requisito adémas de la edad, es que cada votante debe de estar empadronado con la oficina de Registro de Votantes.

27. ¿Qué queremos decir con "el gobierno nacional"?

Queremos decir, el gobierno de un país en el todo en ves de los estados individuales.

28. ¿Se conoce el gobierno nacional por otro nombre?

Si, se llama el gobierno federal que quiere decir que los Estados Unidos son una unión o confederación de estados.

29. ¿Cuales son algunos de los poderes del gobierno nacional?

* proveer para la defensa nacional
* hacer tratos y conducir relaciones con otros países
* reglamentar la inmigración y proveer la naturalización
* reglamentar el comercio con las naciones extranjeras y entre los estados
* acuñar moneda
* colectar impuestos federales, tal como el impuesto sobre los ingresos y el Seguro Social

30. ¿En cuantas ramas se divide el gobierno de los Estados Unidos y cual es la función de cada una?

a. Rama legislativa (El Congreso) que hace las leyes.
b. La rama Ejecutiva (El Presidente) que pone en ejecución las leyes.
c. La rama Judicial (los Tribunales) que interpretan las leyes.

31. ¿Qué quiere decir "checks and balances" (refrenos y balancéos)?

"Checks and balances, quiere decir la forma en la cual las ramas del gobierno comparten del poder para que ninguna

25. How can the Constitution be amended?

Amendments may be proposed by a two-thirds vote of both Houses of Congress or by a national convention called by Congress at the request of two-thirds of the state legislatures. To become law, amendments must then be ratified (approved) by the legislatures of three-fourths of the states or by special convention in three-fourths of the states.

26. How old must a citizen be to vote?

A citizen must be at least 18 years old according to Amendment 26 (1971). Another requirement, besides age, is that every voter be registered with the Registrar of Voters office.

27. What do we mean by "national" government?

We mean the government of the country as a whole, as opposed to individual states.

28. Is the national government called by any other name?

Yes, it is called the "federal" government which means the United States is a union, or federation, of states.

29. What are some of the powers of the national government?
    * provide for the national defense
    * make treaties and conduct relations with other countries
    * regulate immigration and provide for naturalization
    * regulate commerce with foreign nations and among the states
    * coin money
    * collect federal taxes, such as income tax and Social Security.

30. Into how many branches is the government of the United States divided, and what is the function of each?

    a. Legislative Branch (Congress) which makes laws.

    b. Executive Branch (the President) which enforces the laws.

    c. Judicial Branch (Courts) which interprets the laws.

31. What does "checks and balances" mean?

"Checks and balances" means the way the branches of government share power so that no one branch or person can become too powerful and dominate the others.

rama o persona se pueda volver demasiada poderosa y dominar a los demás.

La Rama Legislativa Del Gobierno

32. ¿Cual es el objeto de la rama Legislativa?

La rama legislativa hace las leyes.

33. ¿De que consiste la rama Legislativa que tambien se conoce como el Congreso?

Hay dos "casas" en el Congreso; la Casa de los Representantes y el Senado.

34. ¿Quién hace las leyes federales de los Estados Unidos?

El Congreso hace las leyes.

35. ¿Cuales son las calificaciones mínimas de un representante a la Casa de Representantes?

Un representante tiene que tener al menos 25 años de edad, ser ciudadano de los E.U. por 7 años al menos, y residente del estado en el cual el o ella se elige.

36. ¿Cuantos miembros tiene la Casa de Representantes?

Tiene un total de 435. El número de representantes de cada estado se basa sobre la populación de cada estado.

37. ´Como se eligen los miembros de la Casa de Representantes y cuan largo es su término de puesto?

Se eligen por el pueblo en cada distrito congresional por un término de 2 años.

38. ¿Quién preside sobre la Casa de Representantes?

El Presidente de la Casa que está escogido por los representantes preside sobre sus sesiónes.

39. ¿Cuales son las calificaciones mínimas de un Senador?

Un Senador debe de tener al menos 30 años de edad, ser ciudadano de los E.U.A. por al menos 9 años y residente del estado del cual el o ella se elige.

40. ¿Cuantos Senadores hay?

Hay 100 Senadores, dos de cada estado.

41. ¿Como se eligen los Senadores y por cuanto tiempo es el término de su puesto?

Los Senadores se eligen por voto directo del pueblo de cada estado. Su término en el puesto es de 6 años.

PRINCIPLE OF CHECKS AND BALANCES

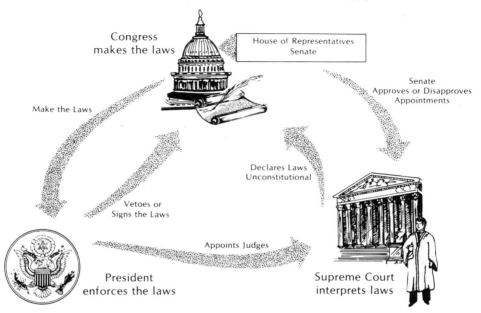

The Legislative Branch of Government

32. What is the purpose of the Legislative branch?

    The legislative branch makes the laws.

33. What makes up the Legislative branch, also known as Congress?

    There are two "houses" of Congress; the House of Representatives, and the Senate.

34. Who makes the federal laws in the United States?

    Congress makes the laws.

35. What are the minimum qualifications of a representative to the House of Representatives?

    A representative must be at least 25 years old, a U.S. citizen for at least 7 years, and a resident of the state in which he or she is elected.

36. How many members are in the House of Representatives?

    There are a total of 435. The number of representatives each state has is based on the population of each state.

37. How are members of the House of Representatives elected and for how long is their term of office?

    They are elected by the people in each congressional district for a term of 2 years.

42. ¿Quién preside sobre el Senado?

El Vice-Presidente de los Estados Unidos es el presidente del Senado y preside sobre sus sesiones.

43. ¿Por qué tiene la Casa de Representantes 435 representantes y el Senado solo tiene 100 senadores?

Los Representantes se eligen segun el número de la gente que existe en el estado, asi es que los estados que tienen una populación más grande, cuentan con más representantes. En el Senado, cada estado, no importe su populación tiene derecho a tener exactamente 2 senadores.

44. ¿Qué es un "Bill"(proyecto de ley)?

Cada ley federal comienza con un "bill" el cual es una propuesta presentada por un legislador (sea un representante o un Senador) al Congreso para que se considere y se le tome alguna acción.

45. ¿Como se hace ley éste "bill"?

Un "bill" se puede presentar ó en la casa ó en el Senado. Si se pasa en una casa, se manda a la otra. Si se vuelve a pasar otra vez, se manda al Presidente para que él lo firme. Despues de que firma el Presidente el "bill", entonces se considera ser una ley.

46. ¿Puede un "bill" hacerse ley sin la firma del Presidente?

Sí, si el Presidente rehusa firmarlo (ésto se llama un veto), regresa el "bill" para atrás a la Casa, y si entonces dos terceras partes votan por el, se vuelve ley. Tambien puede hacerse ley un "bill" si el Presidente no responde al proyecto dentro de diez días.

47. ¿Cuales son algunos de los poderes importantes del Congreso?

* declarar guerra
* proveer el acuño de la moneda y reglamentar su valor
* recaudar y colectar los impuestos

La Rama Ejecutive Del Gobierno

48. ¿Cual es el objeto de la rama Ejecutiva?

La rama Ejecutiva pone en ejecución las leyes.

49. ¿Quién es el ejecutivo principal?

El Presidente de los Estados Unidos es el ejecutivo principal.

38. Who presides over the House of Representatives?

The Speaker of the House, who is chosen by the representatives, presides over its sessions.

39. What are the minimum qualifications of a Senator?

A Senator must be at least 30 years old, at least 9 years a citizen of the U.S.A., and a resident of the state from which he or she is elected.

40. How many Senators are there?

There are 100 Senators, two from each state.

41. How are Senators elected and for how long is their term of office?

Senators are elected by a direct vote of the people in each state. Their term of office is 6 years.

42. Who presides over the Senate?

The Vice President of the United States is President of the Senate and presides over its sessions.

43. Why does the House of Representatives have 435 representatives and the Senate only 100 Senators?

Representatives are elected according to the number of people in a state, so states with a bigger population have more representatives. In the Senate every state, regardless of population, is entitled to exactly 2 Senators.

44. What is a "bill?"

Every federal law begins as a "bill" which is a proposal submitted by a legislator (a representative or Senator) to Congress for consideration and action.

45. How does a bill become a law?

A bill may be introduced in either the House or the Senate. If passed in one house, it is sent to the other. If passed again, it is sent to the President to be signed. After the President signs the bill, it becomes a law.

46. Can a bill become a law without the President's signature?

Yes. If the President refuses to sign (this is called a "veto"), the bill must go back to the House, and if it can be passed by a two-thirds vote it becomes a law. A bill can also become a law if the President does not respond to it within ten days.

50. ¿Quién fue el primer Presidente de los Estados Unidos?

George Washington tomó juramento como nuestro primer presidente en 1789.

51. ¿Cuales son las calificaciones mínimas para el Presidente?

El Presidente de los Estados Unidos debe de tener al menos 35 años de edad, y ser residente de los Estados Unidos por al menos 14 años, y ser nacido en el país.

52. ¿Se elige el Presidente por voto popular del pueblo?

No directamente. El Presidente (y, el Vice-Presidente) se eligen por representantes de cada estado se les llama "electores".

53. ¿Quiénes son los "electores"?

Los electores son hombres y mujeres de cada estado que votan; se les llama a estos votos, votos electorales, los electores votan a nombre de la gente de sus estados repectivos y votan por el Presidente y el Vice-President.

54. ¿Cuantos electores tiene cada estado?

Cada estado tiene electores que equivalen en número al número total de los representantes y senadores que cada tiene.

55. ¿Cual es el número total de los votos electorales que se votan para el Presidente y el Vice-Presidente?

Hay 538 votos electorales, 435 de la Casa de Representantes, 100 del Senado, más tres del Distrito de Colómbia.

56. ¿Cuan largo es el término del puesto del Presidente de los Estados Unidos?

El Presidente se elige por un término de 4 años. La enmienda vigésima-dos a la Constitución, limita a dos términos consecutivos en una vez, al Presidente. Esto quiere decir que al terminarse este tiempo, el mísmo hombre nó puede ser elegido al menos que pase ún término fuera de su puesto.

57. ¿Cuando comienza el Presidente su término de puesto?

El veinte de enero, despues de la elección, el Presidente elegido toma su "Juramento Oficial". Este día se conoce como el "Día de Inauguración", y es el comienzo oficial del término del nuevo presidente.

47. What are some important powers of Congress?
* To declare war
* To provide for coining money and to regulate its value
* To levy and collect taxes

The Executive Branch of Government

48. What is the purpose of the Executive branch?
The Executive branch enforces the laws.

49. Who is the chief executive?
The President of the United States is the chief executive.

50. Who was the first President of the United States?
George Washington was sworn in as our first president in 1789.

51. What are the minimum qualificaton for the President?
The President of the United States must be at least 35 years old, at least 14 years a resident of the United States, and native born.

52. Is the President elected by popular vote of the people?
Not directly. The President (and Vice President) are elected by representatives from each state called "electors."

53. Who are "electors?"
Electors are men and women from each state who cast votes, called electoral votes, on behalf of the people of their respective states, for the President and Vice President.

54. How many electors does each state have?
Each state has electors equal in number to the total number of representatives and senators it has.

55. What is the total number of electoral votes cast for President and Vice President?
There are 538 electoral votes, 435 for the House of Representatives, 100 for the Senate, plus three for the District of Columbia.

56. How long is the term of office for the President of the United States?
A President is elected for a term of 4 years. The 22nd amendment to the Constitution limits the President to two consecutive terms at any one time. This means that after two terms in office, the same man can be elected only by spending at least one term out of office.

58. ¿Cuales son algunos deberes importantes del Presidente?
   * poner en ejecución las leyes federales
   * ser el Comandante y Jefe de las fuerzas armadas en tiempo de guerra
   * nombrar los jueces a la Corte Suprema
   * nombrar a los miembros del gabinete o ministerio (los oficiales ejecutivos del Presidente)
   * hacer tratos con otras naciones
   * otorgarles perdones a personas convictas de crímenes en las cortes federales

59. ¿Puede el Presidente declarar guerra?

   Nó, solo el Congreso puede declarar guerra, pero el Presidente puede ordenarles a las tropas que comienzen acciones sin una declaración formal de guerra.

60. ¿Se puede remover el Presidente durante su término de puesto?

   Sí, a través de la imputación, seguido por un juicio y una convicción.

61. ¿Qué quiere decir "Impeachment" (imputación)?

   La imputación es una acusación de grave malconducta por un oficial del gobierno en el desempeño de sus deberes públicos.

62. ¿Quién tiene el poder de enjuiciar a un oficial federal que sea imputado?

   Solamente el Senado puede enjuiciar un oficial del gobierno que esté acusado o imputado.

63. ¿Quién tiene el poder de imputación sobre un oficial federal?

   La Casa de Representantes solamente tiene el poder de imputar (acusar).

64. ¿Qué es el "Gabinete" (Ministerio)?

   El Gabinete se forma de un grupo de aconsejeros al Presidente. Cada oficial del Gabinete es el jefe de uno de los departamentos ejecutivos.

65. ¿Qué son algunos de los jefes de departamentos que ejercen en el Gabinete?

   Algunos son: el Secretario de Estado, el Secretario de la Tesorería, el Secretario de la Defensa, el Procurador General, el Secretario del Interior, el Secretario de la Acricultura, el Secretario de Transportación.

57. When does the President begin the term of office?

On January 20th, following the election, the elected President takes the "Oath of Office." This is called "Inauguration Day," and is the official beginning of the new president's term.

58. What are some important duties of the President?

* To enforce federal laws
* To be Commander-in-Chief of the armed forces in times of war
* To appoint justices of Supreme Court
* To appoint cabinet members (the President's executive officers)
* To make treaties with other nations
* To grant pardons to persons convicted of crimes in federal courts.

59. Can the President declare war?

No, only Congress can declare war, but the President can order troops into action without a formal declaration of war.

60. Can the President be removed during his or her term of office?

Yes, by impeachment, followed by trial and conviction.

61. What does "impeachment" mean?

Impeachment is an accusation of serious misconduct by a government official in the performance of his or her public duties.

62. Who has the power of impeachment of a federal official?

The House of Representatives, alone, has the power to impeach (accuse).

63. Who has the power to try an impeached official?

Only the Senate can try an accused, or impeached, federal government official.

64. What is the "Cabinet?"

The Cabinet is made up of a group of advisors to the President. Each Cabinet officer heads one of the executive departments.

65. What are some of these department heads who sit in the Cabinet?

Some are: Secretary of State, Secretary of the Treasury, Secretary of Defense, Attorney General, Secretary of the Interior, Secretary of Agriculture, Secretary of Transportation.

66. ¿Como se hace una persona un miembro del Gabinete?

Los miembros del Gabinete se nombran por el Presidente con el consentimiento del Senado.

67. ¿Quién toma el lugar del Presidente si a caso no puede terminar su término de puesto?

El Vice-Presidente tomará la carga del Presidente en caso de la muerte del Presidente, o, si se le remueve de su puesto. Luego sigue, el Vice-Presidente, el Presidente de la Casa y despues de él, sigue el Presidente (pro-tempore, quiere decir por el mientras tanto) del Senado.

68. ¿Cuantos Presidentes hemos tenido hasta é incluyendo a Ronald Reagan?

El Presidente, Ronald Reagan es el cuadragésimo presidente de los Estados Unidos.

La Rama Judicial Del Gobierno

69. ¿Qué objeto tiene la rama judicial?

La rama Judicial interpreta las leyes federales.

70. ¿Cual es el tribunal más alto de los Estados Unidos?

La Corte Suprema es el Tribunal más alto de toda la tierra.

71. ¿Cuando está en sesión la Corte Suprema?

Normalmente se reúne de octubre a junio.

72. ¿Adonde se reúne la Corte Suprema?

Se reúne en el Edificio de la Corte Suprema en Washington, D.C.

73. ¿Cuantos miembros tiene la Corte Suprema?

Tiene un total de 9 miembros. Uno de ellos es el Juez Principal, más 8 sócios, que se sientan como un grupo a oir causas y decidirlas por voto de la mayoriá de los jueces.

74. ¿Como puede hacerse una persona un juez de la Corte Suprema? Por cuanto tiempo es su término?

Los jueces son nombrados por el Presidente por vida, pero el Senado debe de aprobar los nombramientos.

75. ¿Cual es uno de los más importantes deberes de los jueces de la Corte Suprema?

Los jueces deciden si las leyes pasadas por el Congreso concuerdan con la Constitución.

66. How does a person become a Cabinet member?

> Cabinet members are appointed by the President with the consent of the Senate.

67. Who takes the President's place if he cannot finish his term of office?

> The Vice President shall carry out the duties of the President upon the President's death or removal from office. Next in line after the Vice President is the Speaker of the House and after the Speaker is the President (pro tempore) meaning "for the time being" of the Senate.

68. How many Presidents have we had up to and including Ronald Reagan?

> President Ronald Reagan became the 40th President of the United States.

The Judicial Branch of Government

69. What is the purpose of the Judicial branch?

> The Judicial branch interprets the federal laws.

70. What is the highest court in the United States?

> The Supreme Court is the highest court of the land.

71. When is the Supreme court in session?

> It usually meets from October to June.

72. Where does the Supreme Court meet?

> It meets in the Supreme Court Building in Washington, D.C.

73. How many members has the Supreme Court?

> It has a total of 9 members. One of them is Chief Justice, plus 8 associates, who sit as a group, hear cases, and decide them by a majority vote of the justices.

74. How does a person become a Supreme Court justice and for how long is the term?

> The justices are appointed by the President for life, but the Senate must approve the appointments.

75. What is one of the most important duties of the Supreme Court justices?

> The justices decide whether laws passed by Congress agree with the Constitution.

76. ¿Tiene el Congreso poder sobre la Corte Suprema?

Si, el Congreso determina el número de jueces y les fija su sueldo.

77. ¿Además de la Corte Suprema, hay algunas otras cortes federales?

Si, el Congreso usó su autorización recibida de la Constitución para establecer un sistema de cortes federales más bajas que consisten de, cortes del distrito y cortes de circuito.

78. ¿Quién nombra los jueces federales?

El Presidente los nombra con el consentimiento del Senado.

79. ¿Como se le puede remover a un juez federal de su puesto?

Un juez federal se puede remover solamente por el Congreso y al imputarlo y probarlo culpable de crímenes o delitos menores igual que un oficial público.

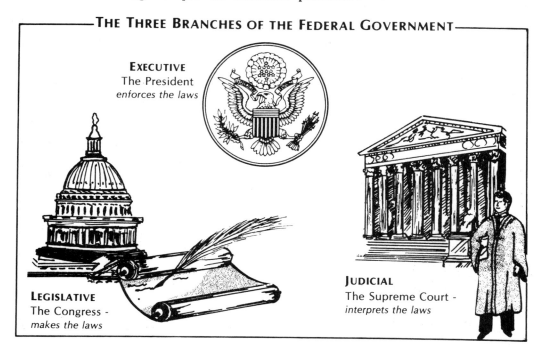

THE THREE BRANCHES OF THE FEDERAL GOVERNMENT

EXECUTIVE
The President
enforces the laws

JUDICIAL
The Supreme Court -
interprets the laws

LEGISLATIVE
The Congress -
makes the laws

La Guerra Entre Los Estados -- Guerra Civil

80. ¿Quién fué el Presidente durante la Guerra Civil?

Abraham Lincoln o, el "Abe Honesto" come se conociá por sus compatriotas, fue presidente durante la Guerra Civil. Fué el décimosexto presidente de los Estados Unidos.

76. Does Congress have any power over the Supreme Court?

Yes. Congress determines the number of justices, and fixes their pay.

77. Besides the Supreme Court, are there any other Federal courts?

Yes. Congress used the authority given to it by the Constitution to establish a system of lower Federal courts, consisting of district courts and circuit courts.

78. Who appoints Federal judges?

The President appoints them with the consent of the Senate.

79. How can a federal judge be removed from office?

A Federal judge can be removed only by Congress, by being impeached and convicted for crimes or misdemeanors as a public official.

ORGANIZATION OF FEDERAL, STATE AND CITY GOVERNMENTS			
	FEDERAL	STATE	CITY
EXECUTIVE BRANCH	President Vice President and President's Cabinet	Governor and Governor's Assistants	Mayor City Manager or City Commissioner and Assistants
LEGISLATIVE BRANCH	— Congress — House of Representatives and Senate	State Legislature Two Houses in all States except Nebraska	City Council or Commission
JUDICIAL BRANCH	Supreme Court Federal Court	State Courts	City Courts

The War Between the States – The Civil War

80. Who was President during the Civil War?

Abraham Lincoln or "Honest Abe," as he was known to his fellow countrymen, was President during the Civil War. He was the 16th President of the U.S.A.

81. ¿Cuando comenzó la Guerra Civil y cuando se terminó, y que fue su causa?

Comenzó en 1861 sobre el pleito de la esclavitud y la doctrina de los "Derechos Estatales", que quería decir el derecho de los dueños de las fincas en los estados sudeños de ser dueños de esclavos. La guerra se terminó en 1865.

82. ¿Cuando y porqué se introdujo la esclavitud a la América?

En 1619, los mercantes Holandéses de esclavos trajeron de la Africa a ésta gente y los vendieron a los primeros colonos. Los granjeros de Virginia y otras partes del Sur los deseaban como obreros para sus fincas.

83. ¿Cual fue el resultado de la Guerra Civil?

Que se revocara la Esclavitud en 1863 con la "Proclamación de Emancipación" de Abraham Lincoln. Entonces en 1865, la Enmienda 13 se añadió a la Constitución revocando la esclavitud. Se conservó la unión de los Estados Unidos de América.

Gobiernos Estatales Y Municipales

84. ¿Como se gobiernan los 50 estados?

Cada estado tiene su gobierno separado y se gobierna bajo su própia constitución. La constitución de un estado nó puede estar en conflicto en ninguna manera con la Constitución de los Estados Unidos.

85. ¿Cuales son algunos de los poderes de los gobiernos estatales?

* Proveer escuelas
* Proteger la vida y la propiedad
* Proveer la salubridad y el bienestar de sus ciudadanos
* Reglamentar la organización y el labor de negocios, de las corporaciones y sus condiciones de trabajo.

86. ¿Quién formó la constitución estatal de cada estado?

Se formaron por la gente de cada estado a través de sus representantes elegidos.

87. ¿Quién hace las leyes estatales?

La legislatura del estado hace las leyes.

81. When did the Civil War begin and end, and what was its cause?
It began in 1861 over the issue of slavery and the doctrine of "States Rights," meaning the rights of plantation owners in Southern states to own slaves. The war ended in 1865.

82. When and why was slavery introduced in America?
In 1619, Dutch slave traders brought people from Africa and sold them to the early colonists. The farmers in Virginia and other parts of the South wanted them for laborers on their plantations.

83. What was the result of the Civil War?
Slavery was abolished in 1863 with Abraham Lincoln's "Emancipation Proclamation." Then in 1865, Amendment 13 was added to the Constitution abolishing slavery. The union of the United States of America was preserved.

State and City Governments

84. How are each of the 50 states governed?
Each state has its own separate government and is governed under its own constitution. A state constitution may not in any way conflict with the Constitution of the United States.

85. What are some of the powers of the state governments?
   * To provide schools
   * To protect life and property
   * To provide for the health and welfare of its citizens
   * To regulate the organization and work of business, corporations, working conditions
   * To make laws regarding such things as unemployment, disability insurance and workmen's compensation.

86. Who formed the state constitution in each state?
They were formed by the people of each state through their elected representatives.

87. Who makes the state laws?
The state legislature makes laws.

88. How are state legislators elected?
The legislators are elected by direct vote of the people of each state.

89. Which is the most important office in state government?
The governor is the chief executive of the state.

88. ¿Como se eligen los legisladores estatales?

    Los legisladores se eligen por voto directo del pueblo de cada estado.

89. ¿Cual es el puesto más importante del gobierno estatal?

    El gobernador es el ejecutivo principal del estado.

90. ¿Por quién y por cuanto tiempo se eligen los gobernadores?

    Los gobernadores se eligen por la gente de cada estado por un término de 4 años.

91. ¿Quién preside sobre el senado del estado?

    El Teniente-gobernador preside.

92. ¿Qué otra forma de gobierno local existe?

    Además de los gobiernos del condado y la ciudad, el municipio y el pueblito tambien pueden tener una unidad de gobierno local.

93. ¿El condado es un gobierno importante local en muchos estados; quien está a cargo del gobierno del condado?

    Una Cámara de supervisores o comisionados normalmente está a cargo del gobierno del condado.

94. ¿Quién encabeza el gobierno municipal?

    El alcalde o gerente municipal encabeza el gobierno municipal.

95. ¿Quién hace las leyes y los reglamentos locales de una ciudad?

    El Consejo Municipal las hace.

96. ¿Como se llama la constitución de una ciudad y como se llaman las leyes municipales?

    La constitución se llama un "charter"(la carta) y las leyes municipales se llaman "Ordinances"(reglamentos).

97. ¿De qué se tratan algunos de los reglamentos comunes?

    * Reglamentos del tránsito y estacionamiento vehiculár
    * La construcción de edificios
    * Tirar la basura

Nuestra Bandera E Himno Nacional

98. ¿Como se llama nuestro himno nacional?

    El "Star-Spangled Banner" (La Bandera con Estrellas)

90. By whom, and for how long, are governors elected?

Governors are elected by the people of each state for a term of 4 years.

91. Who presides over the state senate?

The lieutenant governor presides.

92. What other forms of local government are there?

Besides county and city governments, the town and village may also be a unit of local government.

93. The county is an important local government in most states; who is in charge of the county government?

A board of supervisors or commissioners is usually in charge of the county government.

94. Who is the head of city government?

The mayor or city manager heads city government.

95. Who makes the city's local laws and regulations?

The city council makes them.

96. What is the constitution of a city called, and what are city laws called?

The constitution is called a "charter," and the city laws are called "ordinances."

97. What are some common ordinances about?
* Vehicle traffic and parking regulations
* Construction of buildings
* Disposal of garbage

Our Flag and Anthem

98. What is the name of our national anthem?

The Star-Spangled Banner is our national anthem.

99. What are the colors of the United States Flag, and what do they stand for?

The colors are **red,** which stands for courage, **white,** which stands for **truth,** and **blue** for justice.

100. How many stripes are there on the flag, and what do they stand for?

There are 7 red and 6 white stripes which symbolize the original 13 states.

99. ¿Cuales son los colores de la bandera de los Estados Unidos y que significan?

   Los colores son: rojo, que significa el valor; blanco, que significa la verdad; y, azul, que significa la justicia.

100. ¿Cuantas listas tiene la bandera y que significan?

   Hay 7 listas rojas y 6 listas blancas que simbolizan los 13 estados originales.

101. ¿Cuantas estrellas tiene la bandera de los Estados Unidos?

   Hay 50 estrellas, cada una representa a un estado. La primera bandera de los E.U. tenía 13 estrellas, una para cada uno de los 13 estados originales, y una estrella se añadía cada vez que otro estado para se unia a los Estados Unidos.

102. Dé usted la Promesa de Fidelidad.

   "Prometo fidelidad a la bandera de los Estados Unidos de América y a la Republica que representa, una nación, bajo Dios, indivisible, con libertad y justicia para todos".

   Al conocer las contestaciones de éstas 102 preguntas, leyendo la Constitución en el Apéndice 7, al revisar la fotoscópia que hizo usted de su solicitud, y al sentirse agusto con el inglés, podrá usted completar con éxito el Segundo Paso: La Audiencia Preliminar.

101. How many stars are there on the United States flag?

There are 50 stars, each representing one state. The first United States flag had 13 stars, one for each of the original 13 states, and one star was added each time another state joined the United States.

102. Give the Pledge of Allegiance:

"I pledge allegiance to the flag of the United States of America, and to the Republic for which it stands, one nation under God, indivisible, with liberty and justice for all."

By knowing the answers to these 102 questions, reading the Constitution in Appendix 7, reviewing the photocopy you made of your application, and by feeling comfortable with the English language, you will be able to successfully complete Step Two: The Preliminary Examination.

Capitulo 4
LA AUDIENCIA FINAL

El ultimo paso en el procedimiento de naturalización es la audiencia final. Es un poco formal, pero breve y sencilla. La audiencia final desde luego, es una ceremonia muy importante.

La Ceremonia

Se acostumbraba tener un periodo de espera de 30 días a partir del tiempo cuando se registraba la petición hasta la fecha de la ultima audiencia. Este requisito se ha eliminado por las leyes nuevas de inmigración de los Estados Unidos desde diciembre, 1981 por motivo de eficiencia; asi es que ahora pudiera ser posible recibir un aviso para su comparecencia a su audiencia final en cualquier tiempo despues de que se registre su petición. Sin embargo, usted puede en general, esperar-la espera. En el área adonde vive, éstas audiencias posiblemente tomen lugar solo dos, tres, o cuatro veces en cada año.

El lugar para su audiencia puede o nó ser un tribunal. Depende del juez, que decida él, como acomodar el número de personas que se van a naturalizar en su grupo. Si el grupo es muy grande, la ceremonia puede tomar lugar en un auditorio o en un teátro . En junio de 1981, 9,700 personas fueron naturalizadas en el Coliséo de Los Angeles. No se le exige que traiga a sus hijos a la audiencia final.

Su notificación se parecerá al ejemplar 8. Un escrudiñador de naturalización, posiblemente el que condujo su audiencia preliminar, le informa al juez que usted ha sido calificado para naturalización y debe de hacerlo ciudadano. En general, el juez no le hace preguntas porque el escrudiñador de naturalización yá lo ha hecho. Cuando la corte decide que usted debe de ser hecho ciudadano, entonces usted toma su promesa de fidelidad a los Estados Unidos. Lée en la siguiente forma:

Chapter 4
THE FINAL HEARING

The last step in the naturalization process is the final hearing. It is somewhat formal, yet brief and simple. The final hearing is, of course, a very important ceremony.

The Ceremony

There used to be a 30-day waiting period from the time the petition was filed until the date of the final hearing. This requirement has been eliminated by new immigration laws of the United States as of December, 1981, for purposes of efficiency. So now it could be possible to receive a notice to appear for your final hearing any time after your petition has been filed. However, you can generally expect to wait. In the area where you live, these hearings may only be held two, three, or four times each year.

The place of your hearing may or may not be in a courtroom. It is up to the discretion of the judge as to how to accommodate the number of people in each group to be naturalized. If the group is very large, the ceremony may be held in an auditorium or theater. In June of 1981, 9,700 persons became naturalized in the Los Angeles Coliseum. You are not required to bring your children to the final hearing.

Your notification will resemble Sample 8. A naturalization examiner, possibly the one who conducted your preliminary hearing, informs the judge that you have been found qualified for naturalization and should be made a citizen. Generally, the judge does not ask you questions because the naturalization examiner has already done so. When the court decides that you should be made a citizen, you take an oath of allegiance to the United States. It reads as follows:

La Promesa De Fidelidad

"Con ésto declaro una promesa de que yo absolutamente y enteramente renuncio y descarto toda fidelidad y fe en cualquier príncipe extranjero, potentado, o estado soberano del cual y al cual hasta ahora he sido sujeto o ciudadano; que respaldaré y defendiré la Constitución de los Estados Unidos de América contra todo enemigo del extranjero o doméstico; que tendré fe verdadera y fidelidad al mismo; que aportaré armas a nombre de los Estados Unidos cuando se exija por ley; que prestaré servicio de nócombate en las fuerzas armadas de los Estados Unidos cuando se me exija por ley; y que tomo ésta responsabilidad líbremente sin reservación mental de ninguna clase o motivo esquivatorio, asi séa bajo pena de Dios"

Puesto más sencillamente, el juramento quiere decir: Juro yó, que completamente entrego mi lealtad del país y gobierno del cual he sido hasta ahora ciudadano o sujeto. Doy todo mi lealtad y apoyo todo mi a la Constitución y a las leyes de los Estados Unidos y las obedeceré. Si me llaman, lucharé por los Estados Unidos en sus fuerzas armadas o desempeñaré todo deber que me requiera la ley. Estoy tomando ésta promesa de mi propia y líbre voluntad sin intención de engañar. Asi lo juro ante Dios.

Despues que se ha tomado la promesa, el juez firma la orden otorgando naturalización y cada nuevo ciudadano recibe un Certificado de Naturalización. Este es el documento oficial que ahora lo enseña a usted como ciudadano de los Estados Unidos.

El Certificado de Naturalizacion

Su Certificado de Naturalización se le dará en el tiempo de la ultima audiencia, al menos que sea usted parte de un grupo muy grande que se esté naturalizando. En ése caso, los certificados se tendrían que mandar por correo a cada persona. Si usted pide un cambio de nombre con su petición de naturalización, el juez lo puede asi ordenar en la audiencia final y si es así, su Certificado de Naturalización se expedirá en su nuevo nombre. Cuando lo reciba, sería aconsejable hacer cópia del informe que lleva y guardarlo en un lugar seguro. Es delito federal hacer fotoscópia de un Certificado de

Oath of Allegiance

"I hereby declare, on oath, that I absolutely and entirely renounce and abjure all allegiance and fidelity to any foreign prince, potentate, state or sovereignty, of whom or which I have heretofore been a subject or citizen; that I will support and defend the Constitution and laws of the United States of America against all enemies, foreign and domestic; that I will bear true faith and allegiance to the same; that I will bear arms on behalf of the United States when required by law; that I will perform non-combatant service in the armed forces of the United States when required by law; that I will perform work of national importance under civilian direction when required by law; and that I take this obligation freely without any mental reservation or purpose of evasion; so help me God."

Put more simply, this is what the oath means:
I swear that I give up completely all loyalty to the country and government of which I have up to this time been a citizen or a subject. I will give my full loyalty and support to the Constitution and laws of the United States, and I will obey them. If called upon, I will fight for United States in its armed forces or perform other duties as required by law. I am taking this oath of my own free will and without intent to deceive. I swear this before God.

After the oath has been taken, the judge signs the order granting naturalization, and each new citizen is given a Certificate of Naturalization. This is the official document that shows that you are now a citizen of the United States.

The Certificate of Naturalization

Your Certificate of Naturalization will be given to you at the final hearing, unless you happen to be part of a very large group being naturalized. In this case, the certificates would have to be mailed to each person. If you requested a name change on your petition for naturalization, the judge may order it at the final hearing, and if so, your Certificate of Naturalization will be issued in your new name. When you get it, it is advisable to make a copy of the information on it and keep it in a safe place. It is a federal offense to make a photocopy of a Certificate of Naturalization. That is also why a copy of one does not appear in this book!

Sample 8 - Form N-445
Notification to Appear for Final Hearing

U.S. Department of Justice

Immigration and Naturalization Service

Notice of Final
Naturalization Hearing

OMB No. 1115-0052
Approval Expires 9-30-84

Petition No. _947785_

AR# _A55 416 038_

Date _Dec. 8, 1983_

Pedro Garcia-Gonzalez
621 E. Emmett St.
Santa Ana, California   92707

You are hereby notified to appear for a hearing on your petition for naturalization before a judge of the naturalization court on _December 30, 1983_
at   300 N. Spring St., Los Angeles, California

Please report promptly at _9:30 A._ M.

If the judge finds you qualified for naturalization, you will be sworn in as a citizen.

YOU MUST BRING WITH YOU THE ITEMS MARKED [X] BELOW:

[X] This letter, WITH ALL OF THE QUESTIONS ON THE OTHER SIDE ANSWERED IN INK OR ON A TYPEWRITER.

[X] Alien Registration Receipt Card.

[X] Reentry Permit, or Refugee Travel Document.

[X] Any Immigration documents you may have.

[ ] Your child (children): _____

[ ] Other

Proper attire should be worn in court.

If you cannot come to this hearing, return this notice immediately and state why you cannot appear. In such case, you will be sent another notice of hearing at a later date.

Form N-445
(Rev. 4-15-82)N

(SEE OTHER SIDE)

U.S. Department of Justice
Immigration and Naturalization Service

To Petitioner:

In connection with the hearing to be held on your petition for naturalization, answer each of the questions below "Yes" or "No" without giving any further explanation.

The questions refer only to what has happened after the date you appeared and filed your petition for naturalization. They do not refer to anything that happened before that date.

After you have answered every question, sign your name, give your address, and fill in the date and place of signing.

You must BRING THIS COMPLETED LETTER WITH YOU to the hearing and give it to the naturalization examiner, who will question you further on your answers.

After the date you filed your petition:

1. Have you married, or been widowed, separated, or divorced?
   (If "yes" please bring the proper document, i.e.: marriage certificate, death certificate, divorce decree, separation agreement, etc.)

   (1) Answer ___No___

2. Have you been absent from the United States?

   (2) Answer ___No___

3. Have you knowingly committed any crime or offense, for which you have not been arrested; or have you been arrested, cited, charged, indicted, convicted, fined, or imprisoned for breaking or violating any law or ordinance, including traffic violations?

   (3) Answer ___No___

4. Have you joined any organization, including the Communist Party, or become associated or connected therewith in any way?

   (4) Answer ___No___

5. Have you claimed exemption from military service?

   (5) Answer ___No___

6. Has there been any change in your willingness to bear arms on behalf of the United States; to perform non-combatant service in the armed forces of the United States; to perform work of national importance under civilian direction, if the law requires it?

   (6) Answer ___No___

7. The law provides that a petitioner for naturalization shall not be regarded as a person of good moral character who, at any time after the filing of the petition for naturalization, has advocated in polygamy or been a polygamist; received income mostly from illegal gambling; been a prostitute or procured anyone for prostitution; knowingly and for gain encouraged or helped an alien to enter the United States illegally; been an illicit trafficker in drugs or marihuana, or has been a habitual drunkard. Have you been such a person or committed any of these acts?

   (7) Answer ___No___

I certify that each of the answers shown above were made by me or at my direction, and that they are true and correct.

Signed at _____Santa Ana, California_____ , on __Dec. 15, 1983__
            (City and State)   (Date)

Pedro Garcia-Gonzalez
(Full Signature)

__621 E. Emmett St. Santa Ana__
(Full Address and ZIP Code) California 92707

Naturalización. Por ésta razón, no tenemos cópia de uno
apareciendo en éste libro!

Reemplazo del Certificado

Si su Certificado de Naturalización se pierde, se mutila, o
se destruye, o si su nombre se cambia por orden judicial o por
matrimonio, usted probablemente va a querer un nuevo
certificado. Puede usted solicitar uno al usar el Formulario
N-565 como en el ejemplar 9. Un honorario de $10.00 se le pide.
Mándelo junto con la solicitud.

Una tarjeta de indentificacion

Ya que su Certificado de Naturalización es un papel de valor
que nó se puede fotoscopiar, sería inteligente obtener una
tarjeta conveniente de idenificación tamaño de bolsillo. El
tener una le elimina la necesidad de cargar con su certificado
cuando vuelve a entrar a los Estados Unidos de paises adonde nó
se requiere tener un pasaporte para viajar. Cualquier ciudadano,
sea naturalizado o nacido en el país, puede solicitar ésta
tarjeta. Solo llene uste el Formulario I-196 (el ejemplar 10),
"La Solicitud para Tarjeta de Identificación de Ciudadano de los
E.U.", y adjunte el honorario de $5.00 que se le pide. Una orden
de giro postal o cheque cajero(certificado) se prefiere, pero el
INS aceptará su cheque personal. Vale bien la pena tomar el
tiempo y el esfuerzo (y dar los $5.00), para conservar su
Certificado de Naturalización siempre guardado en un lugar
seguro.

El Significado de la Ciudadania Americana

Cuando complete usted el tercer paso, la audiencia final, y
adquiere su Certificado de Naturalización, al fín será usted
ciudadano de los Estados Unidos. El impacto de su nueva
ciudadanía se puede mejor explicar en el siguiente mensaje del
Comisionado de Inmigración y Naturalización.

Replacement

If your Certificate of Naturalization is lost, mutilated, or destroyed, or if your name is changed by court order or marriage, you will probably want to get a new certificate. You may apply for one using Form N-565, as in Sample 9. A $10.00 fee is required to be sent along with this application.

A Wallet-Size Identification Card

Since your Certificate of Naturalization is a very valuable paper that can not be photocopied, it would be wise to obtain a handy, wallet-size ID dard. Having one eliminates the need to carry your certificate with you when re-entering the United States from countries where a passport is not required for travel. Any citizen, whether naturalized or native born, may apply for this card. Just fill out Form I-196 (Sample 10), "Application for U.S. Citizen Identification Card," and enclose the required $5.00 fee. A money order or cashier's check is preferred, but the INS will accept a personal check. It is well worth the time and effort (and the $5.00) to do this in order to preserve your Certificate of Naturalization by always keeping it in a safe place.

The Meaning of American Citizenship

When you complete step three, the final hearing, and acquire your Certificate of Naturalization, you will have at last become a United States citizen. The impact of your new citizenship might be best stated in the following message by the Commissioner of Immigration and Naturalization.

The Meaning of United States Citizenship

Today you have become a citizen of the United States of America. You are no longer an Englishman, a Frenchman, an Italian, a Pole. Neither are you a hyphenated American -- a Polish-American, an Italian-American. You are no longer a subject of a government. Henceforth, you are an integral part of this Government -- a freeman -- a Citizen of the United States of America.

Sample 9 - Form N-565
Application for Naturalization or Citizenship Paper

UNITED STATES DEPARTMENT OF JUSTICE
Immigration and Naturalization Service

Form Approved
OMB No. 43-R0099

Alien Registration
No. _____

APPLICATION FOR A NEW NATURALIZATION OR CITIZENSHIP PAPER

Fee Stamp

Take or mail to
IMMIGRATION AND NATURALIZATION SERVICE,

I hereby apply for a new: ☐ Certificate of Citizenship ☒ Certificate of Naturalization ☐ Certificate of Repatriation ☐ Declaration of Intention.

(1)(a) My full, true name is __John William Brand__
(b) The name in which my paper was issued was __John William Brand__
(c) Other names I have used are __Johannes Wilhemus Brand__
(2) I now reside at __1121 Avenida del Vista__ __Corona,__ __Riverside Co.,__ __California__ __91720__
    (Apt. No.)   (Number and street)   (City or town)   (County)   (State)   (Zip Code)
(3) I was born at __Kampen,__ __Netherlands__ on __May 17,__ __1926__
    (City or town)   (Country)   (Month)   (Day)   (Year)
(4) I arrived in the United States at __New York, New York__ on __Dec. 7, 1949__
    (City or town)   (State)   (Month)   (Day)   (Year)
(5a) My personal description is: Sex __Male__ ; complexion __Light__ ; color of eyes __Green__ ;
color of hair __Blond__ ; height __5__ feet __10__ inches; weight __170__ pounds; visible distinctive
marks __none__ __Netherlands__ marital status __married__ ;
(5b) Country of which I was a citizen, subject, or national __Netherlands__
(6) The naturalization or citizenship paper was issued to me by __U.S.A. District Court__
    ("Immigration & Naturalization Service" or name of court)
at __Los Angeles,__ __Los Angeles Co.,__ __California__ on __Feb.__ __3__ __1978__
    (City or town)   (County)   (State)   (Month)   (Day)   (Year)
(7) (If applicable) Since becoming a citizen, I ☐ have ☒ have not lost my citizenship in any manner.
(8) Since the date the naturalization or citizenship paper was issued to me I have not been absent from the United States for more than six months, except as follows: (If none, state "none.")

DEPARTED FROM THE UNITED STATES			RETURNED TO THE UNITED STATES		
Port	Date (Month, Day, Year)	Vessel, or Other Means of Conveyance	Port	Date (Month, Day, Year)	Vessel, or Other Means of Conveyance
Los Angeles	11-5-79	TWA	New York	6-10-80	TWA

(9) (If applicable) Such paper became ☒ Lost ☐ Mutilated ☐ Destroyed on or about __12__ __31__ __82__
    (Month)   (Day)   (Year)
at __Corona,__ __California__ under the following circumstances: __Have not__
    (City or town)   (State or country)
__been able to locate certificate since moving into my present address, may have
lost it while moving.__

In addition to the above, answer Number 10 if you are applying for a new certificate in a changed name.

(10) My name was changed to my present name by —
(a) Marriage at __Not applicable__ on _____
    (City or town)   (County)   (State)   (Date)
(b) Decree of __Naturalization__ Court, at __Los Angeles,__
    (City or town)
__Los Angeles__ __California__ on __Feb. 3, 1978__
    (County)   (State)   (Month)   (Day)   (Year)

Signature of person preparing form, if other than applicant	Signature of Applicant
I declare that this document was prepared by me at the request of the applicant and is based on all information of which I have any knowledge. Signature:	*John William Brand*
	Mailing Address: Number, Street, City, State, and Zip Code 1121 Avenida del Vista, Corona, Ca. 91720
Address Date	Telephone Number 714) 544-3174

Form N-565 (Rev.11-26-79)N

AMERICA IS HER FLAG

NAME *(Last in caps)*	*(First)*	*(Middle)*	SNDX
BRAND,	John	William	

PRESENT HOME ADDRESS
1121 Avenida del Vista, Corona, Calif. 91720

BIRTHDATE	BIRTHPLACE
May 17, 1926	Kampen, Netherlands

HEIGHT	HAIR	EYES	WEIGHT	MARKS
5 FT 10 IN.	Blond	Green	170 LBS.	None

FATHER'S NAME IN FULL	MOTHER'S MAIDEN NAME IN FULL
Hendrik Brand	Elizabeth DeJager

I claim to be a citizen of the United States for the reason shown below. I have never to the best of knowledge lost my United States citizenship, in any manner. I ☐ have ☐ have not been previously issued a United States citizen identification card. (If you ever had such a card, see instruction 2.)

☐ Birth in United States ☒ By own naturalization ☐ _____

☐ Naturalization of my parent(s) ☐ Birth abroad of U. S. citizen parent(s).

In support of my application, I submit the following documents:
I hereby make application for a U. S. citizen identification card, and furnish the above information under oath. Signature of Applicant *John William Brand*

FORM 1-196
(Rev. 10-26-79) Y   APPLICATION FOR U. S. CITIZEN IDENTIFICATION CARD   ORIGINAL

Sample 10 - Form I-196
Application for U.S. Citizenship Identification Card

AMERICAN HOLIDAYS

New Year's Day
Lincoln's Birthday
Washington's Birthday
Memorial Day
Independence Day
Flag Day
Citizenship Day
Labor Day
Colombus Day
Veterans Day
Election Day
Thanksgiving
Christmas

PRESIDENTS OF THE UNITED STATES

President	Party	Office Term
George Washington	None	1789-1797
John Adams	Fed.	1797-1801
Thomas Jefferson	Rep.[1]	1801-1809
James Madison	Rep.[1]	1809-1817
James Monroe	Rep[1]	1817-1825
John Quincy Adams	Rep[1]	1825-1829
Andrew Jackson	Dem.	1829-1837
Martin Van Buren	Dem.	1837-1841
William Henry Harrison	Whig	1841
John Tyler	Whig	1841-1845
James K. Polk	Dem.	1845-1849
Zachary Taylor	Whig	1849-1850
Millard Fillmore	Whig	1850-1853
Franklin Pierce	Dem.	1853-1857
James Buchanan	Dem.	1857-1861
Abraham Lincoln	Rep.	1861-1865
Andrew Johnson	Rep.	1865-1869
Ulysses S. Grant	Rep.	1869-1877
Rutherford B. Hayes	Rep.	1877-1881
James A. Garfield	Rep.	1881
Chester A. Arthur	Rep.	1881-1885
Grover Cleveland	Dem.	1885-1889
Benjamin Harrison	Rep.	1889-1893
Grover Cleveland	Dem.	1893-1897
William McKinley	Rep.	1897-1901
Theodore Roosevelt	Rep.	1901-1909
William H. Taft	Rep.	1909-1913
Woodrow Wilson	Dem.	1913-1921
Warren G. Harding	Rep.	1921-1923
Calvin Coolidge	Rep.	1923-1929
Herbert C. Hoover	Rep.	1929-1933
Franklin D. Roosevelt	Dem.	1933-1945
Harry S. Truman	Dem.	1945-1953
Dwight D. Eisenhower	Rep.	1953-1961
John F. Kennedy	Dem.	1961-1963
Lyndon B. Johnson	Dem.	1963-1969
Richard M. Nixon	Rep.	1969-1974
Gerald R. Ford	Rep.	1974-1977
James Earl Carter	Dem.	1977-1981
Ronald Reagan	Rep.	1981-

[1] The party is often called the Democratic-Republican party because in the 1820's it became the Democratic party.

El Significado de la Ciudadanía del E.U.

Ahora se ha hecho usted ciudadano de los Estados Unidos de América. Yá no es usted Inglés, Francés, Italiáno, o Polaco. Tampoco es usted un Americano enlazado -- Polaco-Americano, Italo-Americano. Yá no es usted sujeto de un gobierno. De hoy en adelante, es usted una parte íntegra de éste Gobierno -- un hombre líbre -- un Ciudadano de los Estados Unidos de América.

Esta ciudadanía la cual se le ha conferido a usted solemnemente, es una cosa del espíritu, nó de la carne. Cuando usted dió su Promesa de Fidelidad a la Constitución de los Estados Unidos, reclamó por si mismo los derechos inajenables que se asientan en ése documento sagrado como los derechos naturales de todos los hombres. Usted ha hecho sacrificios para llegar a éste fin deseado. Nosotros, sus ciudadanos compatriotas, lo reconocemos, y el calor con el cual le damos la bienvenida se aumenta proporcionalmente. Sin embargo, queremos tintarlo con un advertimiento amistuoso.

Como ha aprendido durante éstos años de su preparación, éste gran honor carga con la obligación que tiene usted de luchar por, y asegurar éste estado civil tan anhelado y el que usted ha buscado con tanto ánimo. El Gobierno bajo nuestra constitución hace la ciudadanía Americana el previlegio más alto y al mismo tiempo la responsabilidad más grande de cualquier ciudadaniá del Mundo.

Los derechos importantes que goza usted ahora y los deberes y las reponsabilidades que lo acompañan se asientan en otra parte de éste librillo de recuerdo. Esperamos que le servirán como un recuerdo constante de que solo al continuar sus estudios, y aprender más de su nuevo país, sus ideales, sus hazañas y sus objetivos, y, al trabajar siempre mejorando su ciudadanía, que usted gozará de sus frutos y asegurará su conservación para las generaciones que vienen.

Que pueda usted encontrar en ésta Nación el cumplimiento de sus sueños de paz y seguridad, y que la América en su turno nó lo encuentre faltando en su nuevo y orgulloso papel de Ciudadano de los Estados dos Unidos.

This citizenship, which has been solemnly conferred on you, is a thing of the spirit -- not of the flesh. When you took the oath of allegiance to the Constitution of the United States you claimed for yourself the God-given unalienable rights which that sacred document sets forth as the natural right of all men.

You have made sacrifices to reach this desired goal. We, your fellow citizens, realize this, and the warmth of our welcome to you is increased proportionately. However, we would tincture it with friendly caution.

As you have learned during these years of preparation, this great honor carries with it the duty to work for and make secure this longed-for and eagerly-sought status. Government under our Constitution makes American citizenship the highest privilege and at the same time the greatest responsibility of any citizenship in the world.

The important rights that are now yours and the duties and responsibilities attendant thereon are set forth elsewhere in this souvenir booklet. It is hoped that they will serve as a constant reminder that only by continuing to study and learn about your new Country, its ideals, achievements, and goals, and by everlastingly working at your citizenship can you enjoy its fruits and assure their preservation for generations to follow.

May you find in this Nation the fulfillment of your dreams of peace and security, and may America, in turn, never find you wanting in your new and proud role of Citizen of the United States.

Capitulo 5
AL FIN - LA CIUDADANIA ESTADOUNIDENSA

Ya que se haga un ciudadano, puede usted disfrutar de los beneficios de la ciudadanía del E.U. Estos se le escribieron en la lista del primer capítulo de éste libro bajo, "Cuales son los Beneficios?". Un beneficio importante es la calificafición para pasaporte del E.U. Puede usted referirse al Apéndice 8, para ver la Solicitud de Pasaporte, y el Informe para los Solicitantes de Pasaporte. Es importante darse cuenta de que junto con éste beneficio y todos los demás beneficios de la ciudadanía, tambien recibe usted responsabilidades.

Contribuyendo tu parte

Un poder grande de nuestra democracia en América es que, se mortifica de cada ciudadano individual. Cada uno de nosotros tenemos derechos y previlegios garantizados por nuestra Constitución. Cada perona comparte de nuestro gobierno. Su "parte" en el gobierno de los Estados Unidos puede bien ser la contestación en éstas palabras famosa, "....no pregunta que es lo que tu país puede hacer por ti-pregunta que es lo que tu puedes hacer por tu país". El presidente anterior, John F. Kennedy dijo ésto en el discurso de su inauguración.

Votando:

Algo que puede usted hacer por su país es, votar. Es un deber súmamente importante. Cada ciudadano está en libertad de votar en balota secreta por el candidato que quiera escoger. Esta es la forma que tenemos para conservar la democracia de nuestro gobierno bajo el cual vivimos. Franklin D. Roosevelt, otro presidente anterior, una vez dijo que la única forma de garantizar nuestra libertad es teniendo un gobierno suficientemente poderoso para proteger los intereses de toda la

Chapter 5
UNITED STATES CITIZENSHIP AT LAST!

Once you become a citizen, you can enjoy all the benefits of U.S. citizenship. These were listed in Chapter I of this book under "What are the Benefits?" One important benefit is qualification for a U.S. passport. You may wish to refer to Appendix 8 to see the Passport Application and "Information for Passport Applicants." It is important to realize that along with this benefit and all the other benefits of citizenship you get responsibilities, too.

Doing Your Share

One great strength of our democracy in America is its concern for each individual citizen. Each one of us has rights and privileges guaranteed by our Constitution. Each has a share in the government. Your "share" in the United States government might well be the answer to those famous words, "...ask not what your country can do for you - ask what you can do for your country." Former President John F. Kennedy said that at his inauguration.

Voting:

Something you can do for you country is to vote. It is an extremely important duty. Each citizen is free to vote by secret ballot for the candidate of his or her choice. It is the way we preserve the democratic form of government under which we live. Franklin D. Roosevelt, another former President, once said that the only way to guarantee our liberty is to have a government strong enough to protect the interests of all the people, and to have the people strong enough and well enough informed to maintain control over their government. One way for you to exert some control is to vote. It could be your one vote that makes a big difference. Did you know that:

In 1645: ONE VOTE gave Oliver Cromwell control of England.

In 1649: ONE VOTE caused Charles I of England to be executed.

gente, y teniendo un pueblo suficientemente fuerte y bien informado para mantener el control de su gobierno. Una forma para que usted pueda esforzar algun control, es, con el voto. Puede ser el voto suyo el que haga toda la diferencia. Sabía usted que:

En 1645 - UN VOTO le dió a Oliver Cromwell contról de
    Inglaterra

En 1649 - UN VOTO causó la ejecución de Carlos I de
    Inglaterra.

En 1776 - UN VOTO le dió a América el idioma inglés en vez
    del alemán.

En 1839 - UN VOTO eligió a Marcus Morton como gobernador de
    Massachusetts.

En 1876 - UN VOTO salvó al Presidente Andrew Johson de
    imputación

En 1876 - UN VOTO cambió a la Fráncia de la monarquía a una
    república.

En 1923 - UN VOTO le dió a Adolph Hitler su Jefatura del
    Partido Názi.

Cada Voto Sí Cuenta!

Empadronandose Para Votar:

Para votar, usted tiene que registrarse en la comunidad adonde vive. La registración es un procedimiento sencillo. Solo necesita llenar una tarjeta como la que se vé en el ejemplar 11, "Tarjeta de Registración del Votante". Se puede hacer por correo o en persona. Telefonée o vaya a la oficina de Registro de Votantes en su edificio del condado local o el palacio munucipal de su localidad. Tales tarjetas pueden ser un poco diferentes de comunidad a comunidad, pero básicamente, todas requieren el mismo informe. Dése cuenta que usted debe de marcar su afiliación de "partida política", que es a la cual usted pertenece o en la cual usted tiene fe. Si nó lo sabe o si nó quiere usted que sepa nadien, esté seguro de marcar adonde dice, "Rehuso declararlo". Es su previlegio asi hacerlo. Solo nó deje nada en blanco. Marque algo o puede que su tarjeta se le considere incompleta, y que no lo registren. Empadrónese para votar bastante tiempo antes de una elección, ya que hay ciertos límites de tiempo. Es buena idea que se empadrone tan pronto

In 1776: ONE VOTE gave America the English language instead of German.

In 1839: ONE VOTE elected Marcus Morton Governor of Massachusetts.

In 1876: ONE VOTE saved President Andrew Johnson from impeachment.

In 1876: ONE VOTE changed France from a monarchy to a republic

In 1923: ONE VOTE gave Adolph Hitler leadership of the Nazi Party.

Every vote does count!

Registering To Vote:

In order to vote, you must first register in the community where you live. Registration is a very simple process. You need only fill out a card like the one in Sample 11, "Voter Registration Card." It can be done by mail or in person. Either phone or go to the Voter Registration office in your local county building or city hall. Such cards may differ slightly from community to community, but

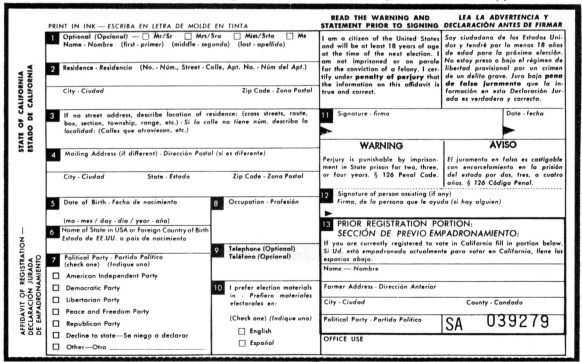

Sample 11

como se haga usted ciudadano, y cada vez que se mueva, tiene que hacerlo todo de nuevo otra vez. Por supuesto, para votar, los ciudadanos deben tener al menos 18 años de edad, segun la Enmienda 26 de nuestra Constitución. El registrarse para votar solo toma unos pocos minutos, y nó puede votar usted al menos que se registre.

Regístrese y infórmese bien. Aprenda algo sobre los candidatos que se postulan. Mire las noticías de la televisión, y léa los periódicos y magazines al menos. Entonces, decida usted quien piensa ser el candidato mejor calificado. El día de la elección, sálga usted a votar!

El Estar Bien Informado:

Además de votar, su "parte" en el gobierno incluye el ser un ciudadano bien informado. Conozca lo que esté sucediendo en su comunidad, en la nación y alrededor del mundo. Se les puede confiar su propio gobierno a las personas bien informadas. Thomas Jefferson, el tercer presidente de nuestro país una vez escribió:

> "... cuando las cosas llegan al punto de estar
> tan mal encarriladas, puede uno contar con que
> la gente, si es que está bien informada, las
> arreglará."

Usted puede expresar su opinión al escribirle a su representante del Congreso o al editor de su periódico local. Su opinión, si es de buen informe, es uno que se basa sobre los hechos.

Además de votar y de ser un ciudadano bien informado, nuestra "parte" incluye el ser leal y tener la buena gana de defender a los E.U.. Debemos de respetar los derechos de otros, obedecer las leyes, y sí, tambien pagar impuestos a cambio de los servicios que recibimos del gobierno. Mucho todavia se tiene que hacer para crear una vida buena para todos en los Estados Unidos. El éxito continuado o el fracaso de ésta gran nación queda en las manos de sus ciudadanos. Este, entoces, es nuestra "parte" nuestro deber, nuestro previlegio.

basically, they all require the same information. Notice that you are to check your "political party" affiliation, the one you belong to or believe in. If you don't know or don't want anyone else to know, be sure to check "Decline to state." It is your privilege to do so. Just don't leave any blanks. Check something or else your card may be considered incomplete, and you won't be registered. Register to vote well in advance of an election, as there are time limits. It's a good idea to register as soon as you become a citizen, and every time you move, you must do so all over again. Of course, in order to vote, citizens must be at least 18 years old according to Amendment 26 of our Constitution. Registering to vote just takes a few minutes, and you can't vote unless you register.

Register and become informed. Learn about the candidates who are running for office. Watch television newscasts and read the newspapers and magazines, at least. Then, decide who you think is the best qualified candidate. On election day, get out and vote!

Being Informed:

Besides voting, your "share" in the government includes being a well-informed citizen. Know what is going on in your community, in the nation, and around the world. People who are well-informed can be trusted with their own government. Thomas Jefferson, our country's third President, once wrote:

> ". . .whenever things get so far wrong as to
> attract their notice, the people, if well informed,
> may be relied on to set them to rights."

You can express your opinion by writing your Congressman or the editor of a local newspaper. Your opinion, if well-informed, is one that is based on facts.

In addition to voting and being informed citizens, our "share" includes being loyal and willing to defend the U.S.A. We must respect the rights of others, obey the laws, and yes, pay taxes in return for the services we receive from government. Much remains to be done in order to create a good life for all in the United States. The continued success, or the failure, of this great nation rests in the hands of all its citizens. This, then, is our "share," our duty, our privilege.

Conociendo a Nuestra America

Haciendo cosas tal como el guardar las fiestas tradicionales nacionales y el recitar nuestra Promesa de Fidelidad en la escuela son solo dos maneras en las cuales usted puede hacerse parte de las costumbres americanas. Léa las páginas que siguen y familiarízese con algunas canciones, simbolos y días de fiesta de nuestro país.

LAS CINCO CUALIDADES DE UN BUEN CIUDADANO*

El Buen Ciudadano aprecia los valores demócratas y basa sus acciones sobre ellos.

El buen ciudadano da su fidelidad a los ideales de la democrácia. Aprecia los valores que concuerdan con la costumbre demócrata de vivir y, vive en el espíritu de éstos valores. Tiene respeto por la dignidad y el valor de la personalidad humana. Tiene fe en la capacidad del hombre para resolver los problemas comunes a través del procedimiento del pensamiento. Se mortifica del bienestar general de toda la gente; tiene fe que la cultura humana les pertenece a todos los hombres. Es leal a los principios de la igualdad de las oportunidades para todos. Todas las características del ciudadano bueno vienen de, y son parte de esta calidad primária.

El Buen Ciudadano practica las relaciones demócratas humanas en su familia, en la escuela, en la comunidad, y en otros foros más grandes.

El buen ciudadano reconoce la interdependencia de toda la gente en su familia, escuela, comunidad, y las relaciones nacionales y mundiales. Practica las clases de relaciones humanas que concuerdan con la sociedad demócrata. Toma a pecho lo que les sucede a otros, así gana el respeto y la confianza. Desarrolla su propia capacidad de cooperar con otros. Sinceramente les desea ayudar a otros. A través de éstas prácticas, edifica la buena voluntad como un recurso del futuro.

Knowing Our America

Doing things like observing traditional national holidays and reciting the Pledge of Allegiance at school are just two ways in which you can become a part of the American way of life. Browse through the following pages and familiarize yourself with some songs, symbols, and holidays of our country.

The Five Qualities Of The Good Citizen*

The Good Citizen cherishes democratic values and bases his actions on them.

The good citizen gives allegiance to the ideals of democracy. He cherishes values which are consistent with the democratic way of life and lives in the spirit of these values. He has respect for the dignity and worth of human personality. He has faith in man's ability to solve common problems through the process of thinking. He is concerned with the general welfare of all people; he believes that human culture belongs to all men. He is loyal to the principles of equality of opportunity for all. All other characteristics of the good citizen stem from, and are a part of this primary quality.

The Good Citizen practices democratic human relationship in the family, school, community, and the larger scenes.

The good citizen recognizes the interdependence of all people in family, school, community, national, and world relationships. He practices the kinds of human relationships that are consistent with a democratic society. He personalizes what happens to others, thereby earning respect and confidence. He develops his own ability to cooperate with others. He sincerely desires to help other persons. Through these practices, he builds good will as a resource for the future.

The Good Citizen recognizes the social problems of the times and has the will and the ability to work toward their solution.

The good citizen recognizes and endeavors to help in the solution of social problems; problems of race, religion, economics, politics-problems of the role of government in

El Buen Ciudadano reconoce los problemas sociales de los tiempos y tiene la voluntad y capacidad de poder luchar hacia su solución.

El buen ciudadano reconoce y trata de ayudar en la resolución de problemas sociales; problemas de raza, de religión, de economía, problemas politicos en el papel del gobierno con relación al pueblo; problemas de los Estados Unidos en su lugar de los asuntos del mundo; problemas del uso equitable de los recursos; problemas de familia, de escuela, de la comunidad y el vivir en el vecindario.

El Buen Ciudadano se da cuenta de y toma la responsabilidad de llenar las necesidades básicas humanas.

El buen ciudadano se da cuenta de la importancia de llenar las necesidades humanas y se mortifica por la extension de lo esencial de la vida para más indivíduos. Toda la gente tiene ciertas necesidades básicas; la necesidad de estar libre de agresiones, dominación, o explotación; la necesidad por el amor y el cariño; la necesidad de pertenecer a grupos y de aceptar ayuda de otros; la necesidad de un nivel de vida que provée una salud adecuada, alojamiento y recreación; la necesidad de tener metas altas de valores espirituales, y éticos de morales. La falta de llenar las necesidades fundamentales humanas puede resultar en el desarrollo del mal-ajuste con el aumento de la intensidad de los problemas sociales.

El Buen Ciudadano tiene en su posesión y usa su conocimiento, habilidades y destreza en una sociedad demócrata.

El buen ciudadano tiene el conocimiento de las capacidades y la destreza a través de su facilidad en la lectura, en el escucho, en las pláticas y en la observación. Usa sus habilidades y capacidades para obtener una comprensión de la estructura presente y el funciónamiento de la sociedad, los principios de los trámites de un gobierno representativo, el impacto de los grupos que ponen presioness, la operación del sistema económico, la categorización de la herencia compleja social. Con su base del conocimiento, de sus capacidades y sus habilidades, el buen ciudadano se vuelve proficiente en la acción cívica.

(*Estudio de la Educación de Ciudadanía de Detroit)

relation to the people; problems of the United States in the place of world affairs; problems of the equitable use of resources; problems of family, school, community, and neighborhood living.

The Good Citizen is aware of and takes responsibility for meeting basic human needs.

The good citizen is aware of the importance of meeting human needs and is concerned with the extension of the essentials of life to more individuals. All people have certain basic human needs; the need to be free from aggression, domination, or exploitation; the need for love and affection; the need to belong to groups and to be helped by others; the need for a level of living which provides for adequate health, housing, and recreation; the need to have high standards of spiritual, ethical, and moral values. The failure to meet these fundamental human needs may result in the development of maladjustments which increase the intensity of social problems.

The Good Citizen possesses and uses knowledge, skills, and abilities necessary in a democratic society.

The good citizen possesses knowledge, skills, and abilities through facility in reading, listening, discussing, and observing. He uses these skills and abilities in order to gain understanding of the present structure and functioning of society, the working principles of representative government, the impact of pressure groups, the operation of the economic system, the social stratification of the population, and the relationship of all these to the complex social heritage. With knowledge, skills, and abilities as a basis, the good citizen becomes more proficient in civic action.

(*Detroit Citizenship Education Study)

DECLARATION OF
INDEPENDENCE

LIBERTY
BELL

El Credo Americano

-- William Tyler Page

Creo en los Estados Unidos de América como un Gobierno del
pueblo, por el pueblo y para el pueblo; cuyos poderes justos
se derivan del consentimiento de los gobernados; una
democrácia en una república; una Nación soberana de muchos
estados soberanos; una Unión perfecta, una e inseparable;
establecida sobre los principios de libertad, igualdad,
justicia y humanidad por cual los patriotas Americanos
sacrificaron sus vidas y sus fortunas.

Por éso, creo que es mi deber a mi país el amarlo, apoyar
su Constitución; obedecer sus leyes; respetar su bandera; y
defenderlo contra todos sus enemigos.

Nuestro Lema Nacional

De acuerdo con la ley Pública Número 851, pasada en la
Segunda sesión del octogésimo-cuarto Congreso de los Estados
Unidos, el 30 de julio de 1956, el Lema Nacional de los
Estados Unidos es: "EN DIOS CONFIAMOS".

The American's Creed
-- William Tyler Page

I BELIEVE in the United States of America as a Government of the people, by the people, for the people; whose just powers are derived from the consent of the governed; a democracy in a republic; a sovereign Nation of many sovereign States; a perfect Union, one and inseparable; established upon those principles of freedom, equality, justice, and humanity for which American patriots sacrificed their lives and fortunes.

I therefore believe it is my duty to my country to love it; to support its Constitution; to obey its laws; to respect its flag; and to defend it against all enemies.

Our National Motto

In accordance with Public Law Number 851, passed at the Second Session of the 84th Congress of the United States, July 30, 1956, the National Motto of the United States is "IN GOD WE TRUST."

THE GREAT SEAL
OF THE UNITED STATES
OF AMERICA

OUR NATIONAL MOTTO
"IN GOD WE TRUST"

Las Fiestas Americanas

El Año Nuevo.......................primero de enero
   (Fiesta legal)

El cumpleaños de Lincoln............12 de febrero
   (Fiesta legal en la mayoría de los estados)

El cumpleaños de Washington
   (Fiesta legal)....................tercer lunes en febrero
   (Tradicionalmente)...............el 22 de febrero

Día Memorial(Demcoración)...........ultimo lunes de mayo
   (Fiesta legal)

Día de la bandera...................14 de junio

Día de la Independecia..............4 de julio
   (Fiesta legal)

Día del Trabajo.....................primer lunes de
   (Fiesta legal)   septiembre

Día de Ciudadanía...................17 de septiembre

Día de Colón........................segundo lunes de octubre
   (Fiesta legal)

Día de los Veteranos................11 de noviembre
   (fiesta legal)

Día de elección.....................primer martes
   (Fiesta legal en algunos estados) despues del primer
                                           lunes en noviembre

Día de dar Grácias..................4° jueves de noviembre
   (fiestas legal)

Navidad.............................25 de diciembre
   (fiesta legal)

American Holidays

New Year's Day...January 1
   (Legal Holiday)

Lincoln's Birthday.................................... February 12
   (Legal holiday in many states)

Washington's Birthday
   (Legal holiday)..................................Third Monday in February
   (Traditional).....................................February 22

Memorial (Decoration) Day...................... Last Monday in May
   (Legal holiday)

Flag Day... June 14

Independence Day.................................. July 4
   (Legal holiday)

Labor Day.. First Monday in September
   (Legal holiday)

Citizenship (Constitution) Day..................September 17

Columbus Day...Second Monday in October
   (Legal holiday)

Veterans' Day.. November 11
   (Legal holiday)

Election Day...First Tuesday after
   (Legal holiday in most states)   the first Monday
                            in November

Thanksgiving Day.....................................Fourth Thursday
   (Legal holiday)   in November

Christmas.. December 25
   (Legal holiday)

Apendice 1
Las excepciones para residencia y los requisitos de presencia fisica

Excepciones Para El Casado(a) Con Ciudadano(a):

Una excepción al requerimiento de 5 años de residencia se hace en el caso de tener esposo(a) ciudadano(a), y puede ser usted elegible a solicitar la ciudadanía despues de solo 3 años. Para hacerse elegible, el extranjero debe de haber estado casado con ciudadano de los Estados Unidos por todo los tres años completos. Un solicitante debe de haber estado físicamente presente en los Estados Unidos al menos 50% del periodo de tiempo para calificarse para la ciudadanía.

Residencia De Los Ultimos Seis Meses:

Inmediatatemente antes de registrar su petición, el solicitante debe de haber sido residente del estado adonde está registrando su petición.

Viajes Afuera Y El Requerimiento De Residencia:

El solicitante nó está obligado a quedarse en los Estados Unidos durante cada día del período de los 5 años. Puede usted hacer visitas cortas afuera de los Estados Unidos sea antes o despues de solicitar la naturalización y puede incluir como parte del requerimiento de la residencia de 5 años, el tiempo que estuvo ausente. Sin embargo, hay límites estrictos para la cantidad de tiempo que se le permite estar afuera:

1. No debe de estar ausente de los Estados Unidos por un periodo constante de un año o más y,
2. No debe usted de estar fuera de los Estados Unidos por un total combinado de más de 30 meses durante los ultimos 5 años.

Appendix 1
Exceptions to Residence and Physical Presence Requirements

Exceptions For A Citizen Spouse:

An exception to the 5 year residency requirement is made in the case of the spouse of a United States citizen, who **may** be eligible to apply for citizenship after only 3 years. In order to be eligible, the alien must have been married to the United States citizen for three years, and the spouse must have been a United States citizen for the entire three years. An applicant must have been physically present in the United States for at least 50% of the time period in order to qualify to apply for citizenship.

Residency For the Last Six Months:

Immediately prior to filing the petition, the applicant must have been a resident of the state where the petition is being filed.

Trips Away and the Residency Requirement:

The applicant is not obliged to stay in the United States during every day of the 5 year period. You can make short visits outside the United States either before or after applying for naturalization, and may include as part of the required 5 years' residence the time you were absent. However, there are strict limitations on the amount of time you can be away:

1. You must not be absent from the United States for a continuous period of one year or more and;
2. You must not be out of the United States for a combined total of more than 30 months during the last 5 years.

Si está ausente por un año o más en cualquier tiempo durante el periodo de 5 años antes de iniciar la petición, esto le rompe su periodo de residencia para la naturalización. Esto es verdad aunque haya obtenido un permiso de volver a entrar del Servicio de Inmigración y Naturalización. Cuando se rompe el periodo de residencia, se tiene que completar despues de regresar usted a los Estados Unidos. Esto quiere decir que tendrá que esperar al menos 4 años y un día despues de regresar antes de iniciar su solicitud. Además, si durante el periodo de los 5 años, usted ha estado ausente por un total de más de 30 meses, entonces tendrá que quedarse en los Estados Unidos hasta que haya permanecido al menos 30 meses de los ultimos 5 años antes de llenar la petición para naturalización en la corte.

Casos Especiales Que Le Disculpan
Su Ausencia De Más De Un Año

En ciertos casos especiales, usted puede conservar su residencia que haya acumulado por motivo de la naturalización, aunque se quede afuera de los Estados Unidos por más tiempo que un año. En estos casos especiales, el tiempo que pasa usted en el extranjero se puede contar como parte de su periodo de residencia. Esta excepción a las reglas generales de residencia es para la gente trabajando en ciertos sectores específicos privados y públicos, y para las organizaciones religiosas.

Para obtener permiso de conservar su residencia, tiene usted que iniciar la solicitud N-470 (véase el ejemplar), antes de salir de los Estados Unidos. En la mayoría de los casos, las personas que buscan conservar su residencia tienen que ser residentes permanentes legales que han vivido en los Estados Unidos por un periodo sin interrupción de al menos un año, con ninguna ausencia de cualquier clase. Los reglamentos son diferentes para los trabajadores religiosos que salen afuera para desempeñar sus deberes religiosos; ellos pueden solicitar al regresar a los Estados Unidos.

Registrando un N-470 no le disculpa al extranjero de su requerimiento de obtener un permiso para volver a entrar en anticipo de cualquier viaje afuera del país de un año o más largo. No le alivia al solicitante de los 30 meses del reqerimiento de presencia física (véase arriba).

If you are absent for one year or more at any time during the 5-year period just before filing the petition, this breaks the naturalization residence period. This is true even if you obtained a re-entry permit from the Immigration and Naturalization Service. When the residence period is broken, a new period of residence will have to be completed after returning to the United States. This means that you will have to wait at least 4 years and one day after coming back before filing your application. Furthermore, if during the 5-year period you have been absent for a total of more than 30 months, you will have to stay in the United States until you have been physically present for at least 30 months out of the last 5 years before filing the petition for naturalization in court.

Special Cases Excusing Absences Over One Year:

In certain special cases, you may be able to preserve residency previously accumulated for naturalization purposes, even when you stay outside the United States for longer than one year. In these special cases, the time spent abroad may be counted as part of the residence period. This exception to the general residence rules is for people working in certain specified U.S. private and public sectors, and religious organizations.

To obtain permission to preserve residency, you have to file an N-470 application (see sample) **before** departing from the United States. In most cases, persons seeking to preserve their residency must be lawful permanent residents who have lived in the United States for an uninterrupted period of at least one year, without any absences whatsoever. The regulations are different for religious workers going abroad to perform religious duties -- they can apply after they return to the United States.

Filing an N-470 does not excuse the alien from the requirement of obtaining a re-entry permit in advance of any trips out of the country of a year or longer. It does not relieve the applicant from the 30 months physical presence requirement (see above).

Miembros Extranjeros De Las Fuerzas Armadas Del E.U.
Y Esposos De Ciudadanos Empleados En El Extranjero

Las excepciones al requerimiento de residencia tocante a las ausencias de un año tambien se hacen para los miembros extranjeros de las fuerzas armadas de los Estados Unidos, y por los esposos de ciudadanos empleados en el extranjero por ciertas organizaciones del E.U. que tienen que acompañar a sus esposos ciudadanos en conexión con tal empleo. Un empleado del gobierno de los Estados Unidos en el extranjero que ha registrado el Formulario N-470, se le considera estar físicamente presente en los Estados Unidos durante se empleo en el extranjero. Un Formulario N-426 (véase el ejemplar) se usa por las personas que estan en elservicio o han prestado servicio honorable en las fuerzas armadas de los Estados Unidos incluyendo sus componentes de la reserva.

Apendice 2
La Provision "Rollback" y los Requisitos de Residencia

Para calificar para la naturalización, los residentes permanentes legales comienzan a contar su tiempo de 5 años que necesitan tener en los Estados Unidos desde el tiempo que sean oficialmente admitidos en este país como residentes permanentes. Hay excepciones a esta regla, sin embargo, que les permite a ciertos grupos de refugiados poder comenzar a acumular la residencia de los 5 años necesitados antes de que sean admitidos oficialmente como residentes permanentes.

El Acto de los Cubanos Refugiados de 1966, el Acto de los Indochinos de 1977, y ciertos refugiados cubridos por la Ley Pública 95-412, adoptada en 1978, incluyen lo que se llama la provisión del "rollback". Esta provisión le permite al Servicio de Inmigración y Naturalización considerar a un refugiado como legalmente admitido para residencia permanente en alguna fecha más antes que la fecha cuando el refugiado recibe su residencia permanente en la realidad. Asi es que un refugiado Cubano o Indochino que se hace residente permanente y mas tarde busca

**Alien Members of the U.S. Armed Forces,
and Spouses of Certain Citizens Employed Abroad:**

Exceptions to the residency requirement regarding absences for more than one year are also made for alien members of the United States armed forces, and for spouses of citizens employed abroad by certain U.S. organizations who must accompany their citizen spouses in connection with such employment. An employee of the United States government abroad, who has filed Form N-470, is considered as being physically present in the United States during such employment abroad. A Form N-426 (see sample) is used by persons who are serving or have served honorably under specific conditions in the United States armed forces, including the reserve components.

Appendix 2
The Rollback Provision and Residency Requirements

To qualify for naturalization, most lawful permanent residents begin counting their required 5 years residence in the United States from the time they are admitted officially to this country as permanent residents. There are exceptions to this rule, however, which permit certain refugee groups to begin accumulating the required 5-year residence **before** they actually become officially admitted as permanent residents.

The Cuban Refugee Act of 1966, the Indochinese Act of 1977, and certain refugees covered by Public Law 95-412, adopted in 1978, include what is called a "rollback" provision. This provision allows the Immigration and Naturalization Service to consider a refugee as having been lawfully admitted for permanent residence at some date earlier than the date the refugee was actually granted permanent residence. Thus, a Cuban or Indochinese refugee who becomes a permanent resident and later seeks to apply for naturalization is given credit for the time spent here as a refugee. Normally, the "rollback" is applied at the time the refugee changes status to permanent resident. However, the law also makes provision to roll back the date on certain other refugees, even after they have become lawful permanent residents.

Form N-470

UNITED STATES DEPARTMENT OF JUSTICE
Immigration and Naturalization Service

Form approved.
OMB No. 43–R0098

APPLICATION TO PRESERVE RESIDENCE FOR NATURALIZATION PURPOSES

(Under Section 316(b) or 317, Immigration and Nationality Act)

(Please read instructions on reverse)

Take or mail to:
Immigration and Naturalization Service

Fee Stamp

Alien Registration No.

Date of Birth   Place of Birth

1. My full true name is ....

2. My home address in the United States is ....
   (Number and street)

   ....
   (City or town)   (State)   (Zip code)

   My foreign address (☐ is ☐ will be) ....
   (Number and street)

   ....
   (City or town)   (State)

3. I am an alien. I was lawfully admitted to the United States for permanent residence at ....
   .... under the name of ....
   (Port of entry)

   on .... on the vessel ....
   (Month)   (Day)   (Year)   (If otherwise than vessel show manner of arrival)

   I have resided in and have been physically present in the United States for an uninterrupted period of at least .... year(s) since such lawful entry. Since the date of my lawful entry, I have been absent from the United States as follows (include date of last departure if now abroad, and if necessary attach an additional sheet to show all absences):

Date of departure	Date and port of return	Name of vessel	Purpose of trip

4. Since becoming a permanent resident, have you ever filed an income tax return as a nonresident alien or otherwise claimed or received benefits as a nonresident alien under the income tax laws? ☐ Yes ☐ No

5. I (☐ am, ☐ will be, ☐ was) employed as, or under contract as, ...

   by ....
   (Name of employer)

   address ....
   (Number and street)   (City or town)   (State)   (Zip code)

   Such employment of contract { necessitates / will necessitate / necessitated } my presence in ....
   (Country or countries)

   from .... to ....
   (Month)   (Day)   (Year)   (Month)   (Day)   (Year)

6. My absence from the United States for such periods (☐ is, ☐ will be, ☐ was):
   - ☐ on behalf of the United States Government.
   - ☐ for the purpose of carrying on scientific research on behalf of an American institution of research.
   - ☐ for the purpose of engaging in the development of foreign trade and commerce of the United States on behalf of an American firm or corporation or a subsidiary thereof engaged in the development of such trade and commerce.
   - ☐ necessary to the protection of the property rights abroad of an American firm or corporation engaged in the development of foreign trade and commerce of the United States.
   - ☐ on behalf of a public international organization of which the United States is a member, by which I was first employed on
     ...., 19........
   - ☐ solely in my capacity as a ☐ clergyman, ☐ missionary, ☐ brother, ☐ nun, or ☐ sister.

7. In support of the foregoing statement of facts I submit the following documents ....
   ....
   (See Instructions)

8. I respectfully request that you find my absence under the above-stated conditions to be in compliance with the provisions of Sec. 316(b) or 317 of the Immigration and Nationality Act.

Signature of Person Preparing Form, If Other Than Applicant	Signature of Applicant
I declare that this document was prepared by me at the request of the applicant and is based on all information of which I have any knowledge.	I certify that the above statements are true and correct to the best of my knowledge and belief.
SIGNATURE	COMPLETE SIGNATURE OF APPLICANT
ADDRESS DATE	MAILING ADDRESS: Number, street, city, State, and ZIP code DATE

Form N–470 (Rev. 11–27–79)N

Form N-426

Form Approved
OMB No. 43-R0265

UNITED STATES DEPARTMENT OF JUSTICE
IMMIGRATION AND NATURALIZATION SERVICE

REQUEST FOR
CERTIFICATION OF MILITARY OR NAVAL SERVICE
(SUBMIT IN TRIPLICATE)

ALIEN REGISTRATION	DATE OF REQUEST
NO. _____	

For use in connection with my petition for naturalization, please complete the certification of military service on the reverse and furnish it to the office of the Immigration and Naturalization Service shown in the address block below. The information shown below is furnished to help locate and identify my military records. APPLICANT: FURNISH AS MUCH INFORMATION AS POSSIBLE. IF YOU WERE ISSUED A REPORT OF SEPARATION, DD FORM 214, ATTACH A COPY. FILL IN THE BLANKS ON THIS PAGE ONLY. PLEASE TYPE OR PRINT CLEARLY. PRESS FIRMLY—ALL COPIES MUST BE LEGIBLE. (DO NOT USE PENCIL)

NAME USED DURING ACTIVE SERVICE (Last, first, middle)	SOCIAL SECURITY NO.	DATE OF BIRTH	PLACE OF BIRTH

For an effective records search, it is important that ALL periods of service be shown below. (Use blank sheet if more space is needed.)

ACTIVE SERVICE:

BRANCH OF SERVICE (Show also last organization if known.)	DATE ENTERED ON ACTIVE DUTY	DATE RELEASED FROM ACTIVE DUTY	CHECK WHICH OFFICER	CHECK WHICH ENLISTED	SERVICE NUMBER DURING THIS PERIOD

RESERVE OR NATIONAL GUARD SERVICE: ⟶ If none, check ☐ None

BRANCH OF SERVICE	CHECK WHICH RESERVE	N GUARD	DATE MEMBERSHIP BEGAN	DATE MEMBERSHIP ENDED	CHECK WHICH OFFICER	ENLISTED	SERVICE NUMBER DURING THIS PERIOD

ARE YOU A MILITARY RETIREE OR FLEET RESERVIST?   ☐ No   ☐ Yes

SIGNATURE (Present Name)	PRESENT ADDRESS (Number, Street, City, State, and ZIP Code)

INSTRUCTIONS TO CERTIFYING OFFICER

Persons who are serving or have served honorably under specified conditions in the armed forces of the United States, inclusive of the reserve components of the armed forces of the United States, are granted certain exemptions from the general requirements for naturalization. The law requires such service to be established by a duly authenticated copy of the records of the executive department having custody of the record of service, showing whether the serviceman served honorably in an active-duty status, a reserve-duty status, or both, and whether each separation from the service was under honorable conditions. For that purpose, the certified statement on the reverse of this form, executed under the seal of your department, is required and should cover not only the period(s) of service shown above, but any other periods of service (active, reserve, or both) rendered by the serviceman.

The reverse of this form should be completed, or the information called for furnished by separate letter, and the form and letter returned to the office of the Immigration and Naturalization Service at the address in the box immediately below.

Immigration and Naturalization Service

◀ RETURN TO

Please type or print complete return address. Include ZIP code.

Form N-426 (Rev.5-12-77)N

solicitar su naturalización, recibe crédito por el tiempo que
paso aquí como refugiado. Normalmente, el "rollback" se aplica
en el tiempo que el refugiado cambia su estado permanente. Sin
embargo la ley tambien hace provisión de voltear para atrás la
fecha de ciertos otros refugiados, hasta cuando se han hecho
residentes permanentes legales.

Los grupos individuales de refugiados son examinados con más
detalle abajo. Si despues de leer este material aquí abajo, que
tenga que ver con su propia situación, usted tiene alguna
pregunta, puede recibir ayuda al llamar a la oficina del INS que
le queda más cerca (véase Apéndice 4).

Los Refugiados Indochinos:
La Ley Publica 95-144 provée el voltear para atrás la fecha de
admisión del refugiado a residencia permanente legal hasta
cualesquiera de lo que viene más al último:
1. 31 de marzo de 1975, o
2. la fecha actual de admisión o libertad condicional, o
3. la fecha actual de admisión del padre u esposo como
   residente permanente legal, si el solicitante es un
   esposo no refugiado, o menor de edad soltero, o una
   persona que se ajustó como refugiado.

Como indicado aquí arriba, es importante que usted comprenda
que al aplicar la provisión del rollback, que úse la fecha mas
última de estas nombradas arriba que en realidad se le puede
aplicar a su caso. Por ejemplo, si un refugiado Indochino entró a
un campamento de reestablecimiento en los Estados Unidos el 10 de
marzo de 1975, pero no fué inspectado y admitido o puesto en
libertad condicional oficialmente por el Servicio de Inmgración y
Naturalización hasta el 5 de agosto de 1975, el rollback no
comenzaría hasta la fecha más última, y naturalmente eso sería el
5 de agosto de 1975. Otro ejemplo, si un refugiado Indochino fue
ajustado como residente permanente legal entre el 31 de marzo y el
28 de octubre de 1977 a traves de los procedemientos regulares de
inmigración y ajuste, esa persona puede solicitar los beneficios
del rollback. La solicitud se hace en el mismo formulario usado
para los ajustes regulares del refugiado Indochino, y debe de ser
completado antes de que inicie el solicitante su naturalización.

Individual refugee groups are examined in more detail below. If, after reading the material below which concerns your own situation, you have any questions, you can get help by calling your nearest INS office (see Appendix 4).

Indochinese Refugees:

Public Law 95-145 provides for the rollback of a refugee's date of admission for lawful permanent residence to whichever of the following comes latest:

1. March 31, 1975, or
2. The actual date of admission or parole, or
3. Date of parent or spouse's admission for lawful permanent residence, if the applicant is a non-refugee spouse, or minor unmarried child, or a person adjusted as a refugee.

As indicated above, it is important for you to understand that in applying the rollback provision, you use the **latest** of the above dates which actually applies in your case. For example, if an Indochinese refugee entered a resettlement camp in the United States on March 10, 1975, but was not inspected and admitted or paroled officially by the Immigration and Naturalization Service until August 5, 1975, the rollback would begin on the later date, which of course would be August 5, 1975. In another example, if an Indochinese refugee was adjusted to lawful permanent residence between March 31, 1975 and October 28, 1977 through the regular immigration and adjustment procedures, that person can apply for the rollback benefits. Application is made on the same form used for the regular Indochinese refugee adjustments, and should be completed before the applicant files for naturalization.

Cuban Refugees:

The Cuban Refugee Act of 1966 provides for the rollback of a refugee's date of admission for lawful permanent residence to the latest of the following dates:

1. Actual date of admission or parole into the United States, or
2. Thirty months before filing an application for adjustment to permanent resident, or
3. May 2, 1964.

Los Refugiados Cubanos:

El Acto de Refugiados Cubanos de 1966 provée un rollback de la fecha de admisión del refugiado como residente permanente a lo más último de las fechas que siguen:

1. la fecha actual de admisión o libertad condicional a los Estados Unidos, o
2. treinta meses antes de iniciar una solicitud para ajuste a residencia permanente, o
3. el 2 de mayo de 1964.

La Ley Pública 95-412:

Bajo la L.P. 95-412, ciertos refugiados con libertad condicional en los Estados Unidos antes del primero de abril de 1980 que adquirieron su estado civil como residente permanente legal bajo alguna otra provisión de la ley, pueden hacer que su fecha se les vuelva para atras hasta la fecha de su libertad condicional original adentro del país.

La Ley Pública 96-212:

Este es el Acto de los Refugiados de 1980, el cual amplifica la definición básica del"refugiado" y le aumenta su admisión a los Estados Unidos anualmente. Tambien contiene una provisión de rollback que las beneficia a las personas que han sido admitidas como refugiados, o quienes despues de su entrada se les ha otorgado estado civil como refugiados. Estas personas no son elegibles a solicitar su estado civil de residente permanente hasta que hayan estado presente físicamente en los Estados Unidos por un año despues de su entrada como refugiado o un año despues de ser clasificados como refugiados. Sin embargo, esta provisión del rollback que les permite a tales personas tener su fecha de residencia permanente legal registrada desde la fecha de su entrada como refugiado, (o en el caso de personas clasificadas como refugiados despues de su entrada a los Estados Unidos) volteada para atrás un año antes de la aprobación de su solicitud para la residencia permanente. Ciertos refugiados admitidos a los Estados Unidos antes del 1 de abril de 1980, pueden ser elegibles para las provisiones del rollback y deben consultar con su oficina del Servicio de Inmigración y Naturalización para aclarecer sus propios casos.

Public Law 95-412:

Under P.L. 95-412, certain refugees paroled into the United States before April 1, 1980, who acquired the status of lawful permanent resident under some other provision of the law, may have their date of permanent residence rolled back to the date of their original parole into the country.

Public Law 96-212:

This is the Refugee Act of 1980, which broadens the basic definition of "refugee" and increases their admission into the United States on an annual basis. It also contains a rollback provision benefiting persons who have been admitted as refugees, or who after entry have been granted status as refugees. These persons are not eligible to apply for permanent resident status until they have been physically present in the United States for one year after entry as a refugee, or one year after being classified as a refugee. However, there is a rollback provision which allows such persons to have their date of lawful permanent residence recorded as of the date of their entry as a refugee, or in the case of persons classified as refugees after entry into the United States, rolled-back one year before approval of their application for permanent residence. Certain refugees admitted to the United States before April 1, 1980, may be eligible for other rollback provisions and should consult their local Immigration and Naturalization Service office for clarification of their cases.

Apendice 3
Reputacion y Lealdad

Como solicitante para la ciudadanía del E.U., usted debe de mostrar haber sido una persona de buena reputación durante todos sus 5 años antes de iniciar su petición de naturalización, y hasta que el juez decida si es calificado para naturalizarse.

La ley declara que no puede ser considerado como tener una reputación buena si es que viene usted de alguna de las siguientes clases en cualquier tiempo durante su periodo de 5 años y hasta que esté verdaderamente naturalizado:

1. costumbre de borrachera
2. polígamo, adultero, personas conectadas con la prostitución o el narcótico, criminales. Un crimen que sea una infracción menor y que no tenga que envolver la "torpeza normal" no le es una barrera a la naturalización
3. los jugadores convictos, personas que reciben su ingreso principal del juego ilegal;
4. personas convictas y encarceladas por 180 días o más;
5. personas que mienten bajo juramento para obtener algun beneficio bajo las leyes de inmigración y naturalización;
6. personas convictas de homicidio en cualquier tiempo.

Las descalificaciones en lista aquí arriba no son las únicas razones por las cuales una persona se le puede encontrar el nó tener una buena reputación. Otras clases de conducta se pueden tomar en consideración por el juez al decidir si un solicitante tiene una buena reputación requerida para volverse ciudadano. Por ejemplo, el juez tiene derecho a considerar las acciones de abuso de criaturas o de esposas, asaltos físicos, obscenidad, el registro de bancarrota o el no pagar sus pagos de manutención de hijos tal como fue ordenado en un divorcio -- cualesquiera que sean contrarias a la moraleja y 'estandards' de la comunidad.

A los extranjeros que no hayan desempeñado sus deberes de servicio en las fuerzas armadas de los Estados Unidos durante un

Appendix 3
Character and Loyalty

As an applicant for U.S. citizenship, you must show that you have been a person of good moral character during all of the 5 years before filing the petition for naturalization, and until the judge decides that you qualify for naturalization.

The law states that you cannot be considered to be of good moral character if you come within any of the following classes at any time during the 5-year period and up until you are actually naturalized:

1. Habitual drunkards;
2. Polygamists, adulterers, persons connected with prostitution or narcotics, criminals. A crime which is only a minor infraction and which does not inolve "moral turpitude" may not be a bar to naturalization.
3. Convicted gamblers, persons getting their principal income from illegal gambling;
4. Persons convicted and jailed for 180 days or more;
5. Persons who lie under oath to gain a benefit under the immigration and naturalization laws;
6. Persons convicted of murder at any time.

The disqualifications listed above are not the only reasons for which a person may be found to lack good moral character. Other types of behavior may be taken into consideration by the judge in deciding whether an applicant has the good moral character required to become a citizen. For example, the judge would be entitled to consider acts of child or spouse abuse, physical assaults, obscenity, filing bankruptcy, or failing to pay child support payments ordered by a court -- any acts which are contrary to mores and standards of the community.

Aliens who have not performed their duties to serve in the armed forces of the United States during a time of war may be

tiempo de guerra se les pueden prohibir la ciudadanía. Esto incluye las personas que hayan sido convictas de haber dejado sin permiso su servicio o de haber esquivado el servicio como a las personas que hayan solicitado y hayan recibido exempciones al servicio basándose sobre el hecho de ser extranjeros.

Es de súma importancia que la pregunta sobre la solicitud tocante al arresto se conteste completamente y correctamente. La falta de revelar un arresto puede resultarle en negarle su petición de naturalización o de revocarle a una persona su naturalización. Todos los arrestos se deben de revelar, a pesar de que el arresto no resulte en una convicción; por ejemplo, si más adelante el arresto fue borrado de su escritura, o si el arresto ocurrió mientras que el solicitante fuese juvenil, o si el arresto ocurrió en otro país o más de cinco años antes de iniciar la petición, o si el arresto fue una violación de un reglamento del tránsito. Los peticionantes pueden desear entregar copias certificados de la orden judicial de los arrestos junto con sus solicitudes para la naturalización.

────────────────────────────────

denied citizenship. These include persons who have been convicted of deserting or evading service as well as persons who applied for and were given exemptions from service on the ground that they were aliens.

It is of extreme importance that the question on the application concerning arrest be answered completely and accurately. Failure to reveal an arrest could result in denial of the petition for naturalization or revocation of a person's naturalization. All arrests should be revealed, even if the arrest does not result in conviction; for example, if the arrest was later expunged from the record, or if the arrest occurred while the applicant was a juvenile, or if the arrest occurred in another country or more than five years before filing of the petition, or if the arrest was only a violation of a traffic regulation. Petitioners may wish to submit certified copies of the court's disposition of their arrest(s) with their applications for naturalization.

Appendix 4
INS Offices in the U.S.A.

The District Offices are listed first, followed by a list of other INS offices. Both lists are arranged alphabetically by **city,** which is underlined. Find the city nearest you to find out where to call or mail for information. When mailing, put "U.S. Immigration Service" at the top of the address.

District Offices

Federal Bldg., U.S. Courthouse
701 C Street, Room D-229
Lock Box 16
Anchorage, Alaska 99513
907/271-5029

Richard A. Russell Federal Bldg.
75 Spring St., N.W., Room 1408
Atlanta, Georgia 30303
404/881-4677

E.A. Garmatz Federal Bldg.
100 So. Hanover Street
Baltimore, Maryland 21201
301/962-2010

John Fitzgerald Kennedy Federal Bldg.
Government Center
Boston, Massachusetts 02203
617/223-2343 or 2344

68 Court Street
Buffalo, New York 14202
716/846-4742

Dirksen Federal Office Bldg.
219 S. Dearborn Street
Chicago, Illinois 60604
312/353-7300

Anthony J. Celebreeze Federal Bldg.
1240 East 9th St., Room 1917
Cleveland, Ohio 44199
216/522-4770

Room 6A21, Federal Building
1100 Commerce Street
Dallas, Texas 75242
214/749-2643

17027 Federal Office Building
Denver, Colorado 80202
303/837-3526

Federal Building
333 Mt. Elliot Street
Detroit, Michigan 48207
313/226-3240

343 U.S. Courthouse
P.O. Box 9398
El Paso, Texas 79984
915/543-7600 or 7601

719 Grimes Avenue
Harlingen, Texas 78550
512/425-7333

900 Asylum Avenue
P.O. Box 1530
Hartford, Connecticut 06105
203/244-2659 or 2699

Federal Building
301 S. Park, Room 512
Drawer 10036
Helena, Montana 59601
406/449-5288

P.O. Box 461
595 Ala Moana Blvd.
Honolulu, Hawaii 96809
808/546-8979 or 8980

Federal Building
515 Rusk Avenue
P.O. Box 61630
Houston, Texas 77208
713/226-4251

324 E. Eleventh Street
Suite 1100
Kansas City, Missouri 64106
816/374-3421

300 North Los Angeles Street
Los Angeles, California 90012
213/688-2780

Room 1324 Federal Building
51 S.W. 1st Avenue
Miami, Florida 33130
305/350-5711

Federal Building
970 Broad Street
Newark, New Jersey 07102
201/645-3350

Postal Services Building
701 Loyola Avenue
New Orleans, Louisiana 70113
504/589-6533

26 Federal Plaza
New York, New York 10007
212/264-5944

Federal Office Building, Room 1008
106 South 15th Street
Omaha, Nebraska 68102
402/221-4651

Room 1321 U.S. Courthouse
Independence Mall West
601 Market Street
Philadelphia, Pennsylvania 19106
215/597-7305

Federal Building
230 North 1st Avenue
Phoenix, Arizona 85025
602/261-3122, -3114, or -3115

76 Pearl Street
P.O. Box 578
Portland, Maine 04112
207/780-3352

Federal Office Building
511 N.W. Broadway
Portland, Oregon 97209
503/221-2271

Federal Building
P.O. Box 591
St. Albans, Vermont 05478
802/524-6742 or 6743

180 East Kellogg Blvd.
932 New Post Office Building
St. Paul, Minnesota 55101
612/725-7115

U.S. Federal Building
727 E. Durango, Suite A301
San Antonio, Texas 78206
512/229-6350

880 Front Street
San Diego, California 92188
714/293-6250

Appraisers Building
630 Sansome Street
San Francisco, California 94111
415/556-2070

G.P.O. Box 5068
Federal Building (Hato Rey)
San Juan, Puerto Rico 00936
809/753-4329, 4379 or 4380

815 Airport Way South
Seattle, Washington 98134
206/442-5950

1025 Vermont Avenue, N.W.
Washington, D.C. 20538
202/724-5756

INS Sub-Offices Which Can Help With Information and Forms

Room 220, Post Office Bldg.
445 Broadway
Albany, New York 12207
518/472-2434,2435, or 2436

Federal Bldg., Room 5512
500 Gold Ave., S.W., Box 567
Albuquerque, New Mexico 87103
505/776-2378

200 E. First Street
P.O. Box 1780
Calexico, California 92231
714/357-1143

Room 600, Federal Building
334 Meeting Street
Charleston, South Carolina 29403
803/724-4350

Charles R. Jonas Federal Bldg.
401 West Trade Street
P.O. Box 31247
Charlotte, North Carolina 28231
704/371-6166

New Federal Bldg., Room 117
P.O. Box 629
Charlotte Amalie, St. Thomas
Virgin Island 00850
809/772-3500

U.S. Post Office & Courthouse
5th and Walnut Streets
P.O. Box 537
Cincinnati, Ohio 45201
513/684-2931

Federal Bldg., U.S. Courthouse
1130 "0" Street
Fresno, California 93721
209/487-5091

P.O. Box 1329
Garden City, Kansas 67846
316/275-1054

104 Federal Building
507 State Street
Hammond, Indiana 46320
219/932-5241

Federal Bldg., U.S. Courthouse
300 Las Vegas Blvd. South
Las Vegas, Nevada 89101
702/385-6251

Room 601, U.S. Courthouse Bldg.
600 Broadway
Louisville, Kentucky 40202
502/582-6375

814 Federal Building
167 N. Main Street
Memphis, Tennessee 38103
901/521-3301

186 Federal Building
517 East Wisconsin Avenue
Milwaukee, Wisconsin 53202
414/291-3565

Norfolk Federal Bldg.
200 Granby Mall, Room 439
Norfolk, Virginia 23510
804/441-3081

Federal Bldg., U.S. Courthouse
Room 4423 N.W. 4th Street
Oklahoma City, Oklahoma 73102
405/231-4121

2130 Federal Building
1000 Liberty Avenue
Pittsburgh, Pennsylvania 15222
412/644-3360

Federal Building, Exchange Terrace
Providence, Rhode Island 02903
401/528-4375

Suite 150, 350 So. Center St.
Reno, Nevada 89502
702/784-5427

410 Old Post Office Bldg.
Rochester, New York 14614
716/263-6273

Federal & U.S. Courthouse Bldg.
Room 1-060, 650 Capitol Mall
Sacramento, California 95814
916/440-3241

U.S. Courthouse & Customhouse
1114 Market Street, Room 423
St. Louis, Missouri 63101
314/425-4532

Room 4103 Federal Building
125 South State Street
Salt Lake City, Utah 84138
801/524-5690 or 5022

701 W. 17th Street
Santa Ana, California 92701
714/836-2327

691 U.S. Courthouse Bldg.
Spokane, Washington 99201
509/456-3824

Room 539
500 Zack Street
Tampa, Florida 33602
813/228-2131

Federal Building
301 W. Congress, Room 8-M
Tucson, Arizona 85701
602/883-5676

Appendix 5
INS Offices Overseas

Note: Some of the addresses below contain an "APO" which stands for "Army or Airforce Post Office." This means that your letter will go by U.S. mail to the APO in the United States, and from there it will be handled by the military to its oversea destination. Mail sent to a Fleet Post Office (FPO) is similarly handled by the Navy. Postage rates are the same as for any mail inside the U.S., and is carried at no extra charge to the final destination.

801 Pacific News Bldg.
P.O. Box DX
238 O'Hara Street
Agana, Guam 96910
472-6411 or 6415

American Embassy
91 Vasilissis Sophias
APO NY 09253
Athens, Greece 09253
71-2951

American Embassy
APO San Francisco 96346
Bangkok, Thailand
252-5040, Ext. 2614 & 2615

American Consulate General
Siesmayerstrasse 21
Box 12, APO NY 09757
6 **Frankfurt/Main,** Germany
74 00 71

Room 39 St. John's Bldg.
Garden Road, Hong Kong
c/o American Consulate, Box 30
FPO, San Francisco, CA 96659
23-9011, Ext. 262 and 337

c/o American Embassy
1201 Roxas Bldg.
APO San Francisco, CA 96528
Manila, Philippines
59-80-11, Ext. 694 or 695

Paseo de la Reforma 305
c/o American Embassy
Apartado Postal 88 Bis
Mexico 5, D.F.
905/553-3333, Ext. 492, 493 or 494

c/o American Consulate General
41 Avenida Constitucion Poniente
Apartado Postal #152
Monterrey, N.L., Mexico
43-06-50, Ext. 27 & 68

Piazza della Republica
c/o American Consulate General
Box 18 FPO NY 09521
Naples, Italy
660-966

Via V. Veneto 119
c/o American Embassy
APO NY 09794
Rome, Italy
4674

c/o American Embassy
APO San Francisco, CA 96301
Seoul, Korea

2 Friedrich Schmidt Platz
c/o American Embassy
1010 Vienna, Austria
346611, Ext. 2355 or 2356

Appendix 6
Information Concerning Citizenship Education to Meet Naturalization Requirements

UNITED STATES DEPARTMENT OF JUSTICE
Immigration and Naturalization Service

Information Bulletin Re: Naturalizations Requirements

A person who is applying for naturalization as a citizen of the United States generally is required to show that he has some knowledge and understanding of the English language and of the history and form of government of the United States. Certain persons are exempted from the English requirements and may become citizens even though they cannot read, write or speak English. The exact requirements, and the exemptions from them, are stated below:

1. The applicant has to be able to speak, read and write simple words in everyday use in the English language.
   Exceptions: A person who is physically unable to speak, read or write English is exempt. The same exemption is given to a person who was over fifty years of age on December 24, 1952, and had been living in the United States for at least twenty years on that date.

2. The applicant has to be able to sign his name in English.
   Exceptions: Those who were over fifty years of age on December 24, 1952, and had been living in the United States for at least twenty years on that date are permitted to sign their names in a foreign language.

3. The applicant has to be familiar with the Constitution and the more important historical facts in the development of the United States, and with the form and principles of our government.
   Exceptions: With the exception of certain former United States citizens and children, all applicants have to show that they have this knowledge. They may show this in a foreign languange if they are exempt from speaking, reading and writing English under paragraph No. 1 above.

The test to determine whether the applicant has the required knowledge of English, history and government is given by a naturalization examiner when the applicant appears before him to file his petition. The test is given orally. The questions asked are in simple English and cover only subjects with which anyone who has made a reasonable effort to learn should be familiar.

Appendix 7

The Constitution of the United States of America

Preamble

WE THE PEOPLE of the United States, in order to form a more perfect Union, establish justice, insure domestic tranquillity, provide for the common defense, promote the general welfare, and secure the blessings of liberty to ourselves and our posterity, do ordain and establish this Constitution for the United States of America.

Article I

Section 1. All legislative powers herein granted shall be vested in a Congress of the United States, which shall consist of a Senate and House of Representatives.

Section 2. The House of Representatives shall be composed of members chosen every second year by the people of the several states, and the electors in each state shall have the qualifications requisite for electors of the most numerous branch of the state legislature.

No person shall be a Representative who shall not have attained to the age of twenty-five years, and been seven years a citizen of the United States, and who shall not, when elected, be an inhabitant of that state in which he shall be chosen.

Representatives and direct taxes shall be apportioned among the several states which may be included within this Union, according to their respective numbers, which shall be determined by adding to the whole number of free persons, including those bound to service for a term of years, and excluding Indians not taxed, three-fifths of all other persons. The actual enumeration shall be made within three years after the first meeting of the Congress of the United States, and within every subsequent term of ten years, in such manner as they shall by law direct. The number of Representatives shall not exceed one for every thirty thousand, but each state shall have at least one representative; and until such enumeration shall be made, the state of New Hampshire shall be entitled to choose three, Massachusetts eight, Rhode Island and Providence Plantations one, Connecticut five, New York six, New Jersey four, Pennsylvania eight, Delaware one, Maryland six, Virginia ten, North Carolina five, South Carolina five, and Georgia three.

When vacancies happen in the representation from any state, the executive authority thereof shall issue writs of election to fill such vacancies.

The House of Representatives shall choose their Speaker and other officers; and shall have the sole power of impeachment.

Section 3. The Senate of the United States shall be composed of two Senators from each state, chosen by the legislature thereof, for six years and each Senator shall have one vote.

Immediately after they shall be assembled in consequence of the first election, they shall be divided as equally as may be into three classes. The seats of the Senators of the first class shall be vacated at the expiration of the second year, of the second class at the expiration of the fourth year, and of the third class at the expiration of the sixth year, so that one-third may be chosen every second year; and if vacancies happen by resignation, or otherwise, during the recess of the legislature of any state, the executive thereof may make temporary appointments until the next meeting of the legislature, which shall then fill such vacancies.

No person shall be a Senator who shall not have attained to the age of thirty years, and been nine years a citizen of the United States, and who shall not, when elected, be an inhabitant of that state for which he shall be chosen.

The Vice President of the United States shall be President of the Senate, but shall have no vote, unless they be equally divided.

The Senate shall choose their other officers, and also a President pro tempore, in the absence of the

Vice President, or when he shall exercise the office of President of the United States.

The Senate shall have the sole power to try all impeachments. When sitting for that purpose, they shall be on oath or affirmation. When the President of the United States is tried, the Chief Justice shall preside: And no person shall be convicted without the concurrence of two-thirds of the members present.

Judgment in cases of impeachment shall not extend further than to removal from office, and disqualification to hold and enjoy any office of honor, trust or profit under the United States: but the party convicted shall nevertheless be liable and subject to indictment, trial, judgment and punishment, according to law.

Section 4. The times, places and manner of holding elections for Senators and Representatives, shall be prescribed in each state by the legislature thereof; but the Congress may at any time by law make or alter such regulations, except as to the places of choosing Senators.

The Congress shall assemble at least once in every year, and such meeting shall be on the first Monday in December, unless they shall by law appoint a different day.

Section 5. Each House shall be the judge of the elections, returns and qualifications of its own members, and a majority of each shall constitute a quorum to do business; but a smaller number may adjourn from day to day, and may be authorized to compel the attendance of absent members, in such manner, and under such penalties as each House may provide.

Each House may determine the rules of its proceedings, punish its members for disorderly behaviour, and, with the concurrence of two-thirds, expel a member.

Each House shall keep a journal of its proceedings, and from time to time publish the same, excepting such parts as may in their judgment require secrecy; and the yeas and nays of the members of either House on any question shall, at the desire of one-fifth of those present, be entered on the journal.

Neither House, during the session of Congress, shall, without the consent of the other, adjourn for more than three days, nor to any other place than that in which the two Houses shall be sitting.

Section 6. The Senators and Representatives shall receive a compensation for their services, to be ascertained by law, and paid out of the Treasury of the United States. They shall in all cases, except treason, felony and breach of the peace, be privileged from arrest during their attendance at the session of their respective Houses, and in going to and returning from the same; and for any speech or debate in either House, they shall not be questioned in any other place.

No Senator or Representative shall, during the time for which he was elected, be appointed to any civil office under the authority of the United States, which shall have been created, or the emoluments whereof shall have been increased during such time; and no person holding any office under the United States, shall be a member of either House during his continuance in office.

Section 7. All bills for raising revenue shall originate in the House of Representatives; but the Senate may propose or concur with amendments as on other bills.

Every bill which shall have passed the House of Representatives and the Senate, shall, before it becomes a law, be presented to the President of the United States; if he approves he shall sign it, but if not he shall return it, with his objections to that House in which it shall have originated, who shall enter the objections at large on their journal, and proceed to reconsider it. If after such reconsideration two thirds of that House shall agree to pass the bill, it shall be sent, together with the objections, to the other House, by which it shall likewise be reconsidered, and if approved by two thirds of that House, it shall become a law. But in all such cases the votes of both Houses shall be determined by yeas and nays, and the names of the persons voting for and against the bill shall be entered on the journal of each House respectively. If any bill shall not be returned by the President within ten days (Sundays excepted) after it shall have been presented to him, the same shall be a law, in like manner as if he had signed it, unless the Congress by their adjournment prevent its return, in which case it shall not be a law.

Every order, resolution, or vote to which the concurrence of the Senate and House of Representatives may be necessary (except on a question of adjournment) shall be presented to the Presi-

dent of the United States; and before the same shall take effect, shall be approved by him, or being disapproved by him, shall be repassed by two thirds of the Senate and House of Representatives, according to the rules and limitations prescribed in the case of a bill.

Section 8. The Congress shall have power to lay and collect taxes, duties, imposts and excises, to pay the debts and provide for the common defense and general welfare of the United States; but all duties, imposts and excises shall be uniform throughout the United States;

To borrow money on the credit of the United States;

To regulate commerce with foreign nations, and among the several States, and with the Indian tribes;

To establish a uniform rule of naturalization, and uniform laws on the subject of bankruptcies throughout the United States;

To coin money, regulate the value thereof, and of foreign coin, and fix the standard of weights and measures;

To provide for the punishment of counterfeiting the securities and current coin of the United States;

To establish post offices and post roads;

To promote the progress of science and useful arts, by securing for limited times to authors and inventors the exclusive right to their respective writings and discoveries;

To constitute tribunals inferior to the Supreme Court;

To define and punish piracies and felonies committed on the high seas, and offenses against the law of nations;

To declare war, grant letters of marque and reprisal, and make rules concerning captures on land and water;

To raise and support armies, but no appropriation of money to that use shall be for a longer term than two years;

To provide and maintain a Navy;

To make rules for the government and regulation of the land and naval forces;

To provide for calling forth the militia to execute the laws of the Union, suppress insurrections and repel invasions;

To provide for organizing, arming, and disciplining, the militia, and for governing such part of them as may be employed in the service of the United States, reserving to the states respectively, the appointment of the officers, and the authority of training the militia according to the discipline prescribed by Congress;

To exercise exclusive legislation in all cases whatsoever, over such District (not exceeding ten miles square) as may, by cession of particular states, and the acceptance of Congress, become the seat of the government of the United States, and to exercise like authority over all places purchased by the consent of the legislature of the state in which the same shall be, for the erection of forts, magazines, arsenals, dock-yards, and other needful buildings;—and

To make all laws which shall be necessary and proper for carrying into execution the foregoing powers, and all other powers vested by this Constitution in the government of the United States, or in any department or officer thereof.

Section 9. The migration or importation of such persons as any of the states now existing shall think proper to admit, shall not be prohibited by the Congress prior to the year one thousand eight hundred and eight, but a tax or duty may be imposed on such importation, not exceeding ten dollars for each person.

The privilege of the writ of habeas corpus shall not be suspended, unless when in cases of rebellion or invasion the public safety may require it.

No bill of attainder or ex post facto law shall be passed.

No capitation, or other direct, tax shall be laid, unless in proportion to the census or enumeration herein before directed to be taken.

No tax or duty shall be laid on articles exported from any state.

No preference shall be given by any regulation of commerce or revenue to the ports of one state over those of another: nor shall vessels bound to, or from, one state, be obliged to enter, clear, or pay duties in another.

No money shall be drawn from the Treasury, but in consequence of appropriations made by law; and a regular statement and account of the receipts and expenditures of all public money shall be published from time to time.

No title of nobility shall be granted by the United States: And no person holding any office of profit or trust under them, shall, without the

consent of the Congress, accept of any present, emolument, office, or title, of any kind whatever, from any King, Prince, or foreign state.

Section 10. No state shall enter into any treaty, alliance, or confederation; grant letters of marque and reprisal; coin money; emit bills of credit; make any thing but gold and silver coin a tender in payment of debts; pass any bill of attainder, ex post facto law, or law impairing the obligation of contracts, or grant any title of nobility.

No state shall, without the consent of the Congress, lay any imposts or duties on imports or exports, except what may be absolutely necessary for executing its inspection laws: and the net produce of all duties and imposts, laid by any state on imports or exports, shall be for the use of the Treasury of the United States; and all such laws shall be subject to the revision and control of the Congress.

No state shall, without the consent of Congress, lay any duty of tonnage, keep troops, or ships of war in time of peace, enter into any agreement or compact with another state, or with a foreign power, or engage in war, unless actually invaded, or in such imminent danger as will not admit of delay.

Article II

Section 1. The executive power shall be vested in a President of the United States of America. He shall hold his office during the term of four years, and, together with the Vice President, chosen for the same term, be elected, as follows:

Each state, shall appoint, in such manner as the legislature thereof may direct, a number of electors, equal to the whole number of Senators and Representatives to which the state may be entitled in the Congress; but no Senator or Representative, or person holding an office of trust or profit under the United States, shall be appointed an elector.

The electors shall meet in their respective states, and vote by ballot for two persons, of whom one at least shall not be an inhabitant of the same state with themselves. And they shall make a list of all the persons voted for, and of the number of votes for each; which list they shall sign and certify, and transmit sealed to the seat of the government of the United States, directed to the President of the Senate. The President of the Senate

shall, in the presence of the Senate and House of Representatives, open all the certificates, and the votes shall then be counted. The person having the greatest number of votes shall be the President, if such number be a majority of the whole number of electors appointed; and if there be more than one who have such majority, and have an equal number of votes, then the House of Representatives shall immediately choose by ballot one of them for President; and if no person have a majority, then from the five highest on the list the said House shall in like manner choose the President. But in choosing the President, the votes shall be taken by states, the representation from each state having one vote; a quorum for this purpose shall consist of a member or members from two thirds of the states, and a majority of all the states shall be necessary to a choice.

In every case, after the choice of the President, the person having the greatest number of votes of the electors shall be the Vice President. But if there should remain two or more who have equal votes, the Senate shall choose from them by ballot the Vice President.

The Congress may determine the time of choosing the electors, and the day on which they shall give their votes; which day shall be the same throughout the United States.

No person except a natural born citizen, or a citizen of the United States, at the time of the adoption of this Constitution, shall be eligible to the office of President; neither shall any person be eligible to that office who shall not have attained to the age of thirty-five years, and been fourteen years a resident within the United States.

In case of the removal of the President from office, or of his death, resignation, or inability to discharge the powers and duties of the said office, the same shall devolve on the Vice President, and the Congress may by law provide for the case of removal, death, resignation, or inability, both of the President and Vice President, declaring what officer shall then act as President, and such officer shall act accordingly, until the disability be removed, or a President shall be elected.

The President shall, at stated times, receive for his services, a compensation, which shall neither be increased nor diminished during the period for which he shall have been elected, and he shall not

receive within that period any other emolument from the United States, or any of them.

Before he enters on the execution of his office, he shall take the following oath or affirmation:—"I do solemnly swear (or affirm) that I will faithfully execute the office of President of the United States, and will to the best of my ability, preserve, protect and defend the Constitution of the United States."

Section 2. The President shall be commander in chief of the Army and Navy of the United States, and of the militia of the several States, when called into the actual service of the United States; he may require the opinion, in writing, of the principal officer in each of the executive departments, upon any subject relating to the duties of their respective offices, and he shall have power to grant reprieves and pardons for offenses against the United States, except in cases of impeachment.

He shall have power, by and with the advice and consent of the Senate, to make treaties, provided two thirds of the Senators present concur; and he shall nominate, and by and with the advice and consent of the Senate, shall appoint ambassadors, other public ministers and consuls, judges of the Supreme Court, and all other officers of the United States, whose appointments are not herein otherwise provided for, and which shall be established by law: but the Congress may by law vest the appointment of such inferior officers, as they think proper, in the President alone, in the courts of law, or in the heads of departments.

The President shall have power to fill up all vacancies that may happen during the recess of the Senate, by granting commissions which shall expire at the end of their next session.

Section 3. He shall from time to time give to the Congress information of the state of the Union, and recommend to their consideration such measures as he shall judge necessary and expedient; he may, on extraordinary occasions, convene both Houses, or either of them, and in case of disagreement between them, with respect to the time of adjournment, he may adjourn them to such time as he shall think proper; he shall receive ambassadors and other public ministers; he shall take care that the laws be faithfully executed, and shall commission all the officers of the United States.

Section 4. The President, Vice President and all civil officers of the United States, shall be removed from office on impeachment for, and conviction of, treason, bribery, or other high crimes and misdemeanors.

Article III

Section 1. The judicial power of the United States, shall be vested in one Supreme Court, and in such inferior courts as the Congress may from time to time ordain and establish. The judges, both of the supreme and inferior courts, shall hold their offices during good behaviour, and shall, at stated times, receive for their services, a compensation, which shall not be diminished during their continuance in office.

Section 2. The judicial power shall extend to all cases, in law and equity, arising under this Constitution, the laws of the United States, and treaties made, or which shall be made, under their authority;—to all cases affecting ambassadors, other public ministers and consuls;—to all cases of admiralty and maritime jurisdiction;—to controversies to which the United States shall be a party;—to controversies between two or more states;—between a state and citizens of another state;—between citizens of different states,—between citizens of the same state claiming lands under grants of different states, and between a state, or the citizens thereof, and foreign states, citizens or subjects.

In all cases affecting ambassadors, other public ministers and consuls, and those in which a state shall be a party, the Supreme Court shall have original jurisdiction. In all the other cases before mentioned, the Supreme Court shall have appellate jurisdiction, both as to law and fact, with such exceptions, and under such regulations as the Congress shall make.

The trial of all crimes, except in cases of impeachment, shall be by jury; and such trial shall be held in the state where the said crimes shall have been committed; but when not committed within any state, the trial shall be at such place or places as the Congress may by law have directed.

Section 3. Treason against the United States, shall consist only in levying war against them, or in adhering to their enemies, giving them aid and comfort. No person shall be convicted of treason unless on the testimony of two witnesses to the same overt act, or on confession in open court.

The Congress shall have power to declare the punishment of treason, but no attainder of treason shall work corruption of blood, or forfeiture except during the life of the person attained.

Article IV

Section 1. Full faith and credit shall be given in each state to the public acts, records, and judicial proceedings of every other state. And the Congress may by general laws prescribe the manner in which such acts, records and proceedings shall be proved, and the effect thereof.

Section 2. The citizens of each state shall be entitled to all privileges and immunities of citizens in the several states.

A person charged in any state with treason, felony, or other crime, who shall flee from justice, and be found in another state, shall on demand of the executive authority of the state from which he fled, be delivered up, to be removed to the state having jurisdiction of the crime.

No person held to service or labour in one state, under the laws thereof, escaping into another, shall, in consequence of any law or regulation therein, be discharged from such service or labour, but shall be delivered up on claim of the party to whom such service or labour may be due.

Section 3. New states may be admitted by the Congress into this Union; but no new state shall be formed or erected within the jurisdiction of any other state; nor any state be formed by the junction of two or more states, or parts of states, without the consent of the legislature of the states concerned as well as of the Congress.

The Congress shall have power to dispose of and make all needful rules and regulations respecting the territory or other property belonging to the United States; and nothing in this Constitution shall be so construed as to prejudice any claims of the United States, or of any particular state.

Section 4. The United States shall guarantee to every state in this Union a republican form of government, and shall protect each of them against invasion; and on application of the legislature, or of the executive (when the legislature cannot be convened) against domestic violence.

Article V

The Congress, whenever two thirds of both Houses shall deem it necessary, shall propose amendments to this Constitution, or on the application of the legislatures of two thirds of the several states, shall call a convention for proposing amendments, which, in either case, shall be valid to all intents and purposes, as part of this Constitution, when ratified by the legislatures of three fourths of the several States, or by conventions in three fourths thereof, as the one or the other mode of ratification may be proposed by the Congress; provided that no amendment which may be made prior to the year one thousand eight hundred and eight shall in any manner affect the first and fourth clauses in the Ninth Section of the First Article; and that no state, without its consent, shall be deprived of its equal suffrage in the Senate.

Article VI

All debts contracted and engagements entered into, before the adoption of this Constitution, shall be as valid against the United States under this Constitution, as under the Confederation.

This Constitution, and the laws of the United States which shall be made in pursuance thereof; and all treaties made, or which shall be made, under the authority of the United States, shall be the supreme law of the land; and the judges in every state shall be bound thereby, any thing in the Constitution or laws of any State to the contrary notwithstanding.

The Senators and Representatives before mentioned, and the members of the several state legislatures, and all executive and judicial officers, both of the United States and of the several states, shall be bound by oath or affirmation, to support this Constitution; but no religious test shall ever be required as a qualification to any office or public trust under the United States.

Article VII

The ratification of the conventions of nine states shall be sufficient for the establishment of this Constitution between the states so ratifying the same.

Done in convention by the unanimous consent of the states present the seventeenth day of September in the year of our Lord one thousand seven

hundred and eighty seven and of the independence of the United States of America the twelfth. In witness whereof we have hereunto subscribed our names,

Go. WASHINGTON—*Presid't,*
and deputy from Virginia
Attest WILLIAM JACKSON *Secretary*

New Hampshire
JOHN LANGDON   NICHOLAS GILMAN

Massachusetts
NATHANIEL GORHAM   RUFUS KING

Connecticut
WM. SAML. JOHNSON   ROGER SHERMAN

New York
ALEXANDER HAMILTON

New Jersey
WIL: LIVINGSTON   WM. PATERSON
DAVID BREARLEY   JONA: DAYTON

Pennsylvania
B FRANKLIN   THOS. FITZSIMONS
THOMAS MIFFLIN   JARED INGERSOLL
ROBT MORRIS   JAMES WILSON
GEO. CLYMER   GOUV MORRIS

Delaware
GEO: READ   RICHARD BASSETT
GUNNING BEDFORD JUN   JACO: BROOM
JOHN DICKINSON

Maryland
JAMES MCHENRY   DANL CARROLL
DAN OF ST THOS. JENIFER

Virginia
JOHN BLAIR—   JAMES MADISON JR.

North Carolina
WM. BLOUNT   HU WILLIAMSON
RICHD. DOBBS SPAIGHT

South Carolina
J. RUTLEDGE   CHARLES PINCKNEY
CHARLES COTESWORTH   PIERCE BUTLER
PINCKNEY

Georgia
WILLIAM FEW   ABR BALDWIN

Amendments

Article I

Congress shall make no law respecting an establishment of religion, or prohibiting the free exercise thereof; or abridging the freedom of speech, or of the press; or the right of the people peaceably to assemble, and to petition the government for a redress of grievances.

Article II

A well-regulated militia, being necessary to the security of a free state, the right of the people to keep and bear arms, shall not be infringed.

Article III

No soldier shall, in time of peace be quartered in any house, without the consent of the owner, nor in time of war, but in a manner to be prescribed by law.

Article IV

Tht right of the people to be secure in their persons, houses, papers, and effects, against unreasonable searches and seizures, shall not be violated, and no warrants shall issue, but upon probable cause, supported by oath or affirmation, and particularly describing the place to be searched, and the persons or things to be seized.

Article V

No person shall be held to answer for a capital, or otherwise infamous crime, unless on a presentment or indictment of a Grand Jury, except in cases arising in the land or naval forces, or in the militia, when in actual service in time of war or public danger; nor shall any person be subject for the same offense to be twice put in jeopardy of life or limb; nor shall be compelled in any criminal case to be a witness against himself, nor be deprived of life, liberty, or property, without due process of law; nor shall private property be taken for public use, without just compensation.

Article VI

In all criminal prosecutions, the accused shall enjoy the right to a speedy and public trial, by an impartial jury of the state and district wherein the crime shall have been committed, which district shall have been previously ascertained by law, and to be informed of the nature and cause of the accusation; to be confronted with the witnesses against him; to have compulsory process for obtaining witnesses in his favor, and to have the assistance of counsel for his defense.

Article VII

In suits at common law, where the value in controversy shall exceed twenty dollars, the right of trial by jury shall be preserved, and no fact tried by a jury, shall be otherwise reexamined in any court of the United States, than according to the rules of the common law.

Article VIII

Excessive bail shall not be required, nor excessive fines imposed, nor cruel and unusual punishments inflicted.

Article IX

The enumeration in the Constitution, of certain rights, shall not be construed to deny or disparage others retained by the people.

Article X

The powers not delegated to the United States by the Constitution, nor prohibited by it to the states, are reserved to the states respectively, or to the people.

Article XI

The judicial power of the United States shall not be construed to extend to any suit in law or equity, commenced or prosecuted against one of the United States by citizens of another state, or by citizens or subjects of any foreign state.

Article XII

The electors shall meet in their respective states, and vote by ballot for President and Vice President, one of whom, at least, shall not be an inhabitant of the same state with themselves; they shall name in their ballots the person voted for as President, and in distinct ballots the person voted for as Vice President, and they shall make distinct lists of all persons voted for as President, and of all persons voted for as Vice President, and of the number of votes for each, which lists they shall sign and certify, and transmit sealed to the seat of the government of the United States, directed to the President of the Senate;—The President of the Senate shall, in the presence of the Senate and House of Representatives, open all the certificates and the votes shall then be counted;—The person having the greatest number of votes for President, shall be the President, if such number be a majority of the whole number of electors appointed; and if no person have such majority, then from the persons having the highest numbers not exceeding three on the list of those voted for as President, the House of Representatives shall choose immediately, by ballot, the President. But in choosing the President, the votes shall be taken by states, the representation from each state having one vote; a quorum for this purpose shall consist of a member or members from two-thirds of the states, and a majority of all the states shall be necessary to a choice. And if the House of Representatives shall not choose a President whenever the right of choice shall devolve upon them, before the fourth day of March next following, then the Vice President shall act as President, as in the case of the death or other constitutional disability of the President.—The person having the greatest number of votes as Vice President, shall be the Vice President, if such number be a majority of the whole number of electors appointed, and if no person have a majority, then from the two highest numbers on the list, the Senate shall choose the Vice President; a quorum for the purpose shall consist of two-thirds of the whole number of Senators, and a majority of the whole number shall be necessary to a choice. But no person constitutionally ineligible to the office of President shall be eligible to that of Vice President of the United States.

Article XIII

Section 1. Neither slavery nor involuntary servitude, except as a punishment for crime whereof the party shall have been duly convicted, shall exist within the United States, or any place subject to their jurisdiction.

Section 2. Congress shall have power to enforce this article by appropriate legislation.

Article XIV

Section 1. All persons born or naturalized in the United States, and subject to the jurisdiction thereof, are citizens of the United States and of the state wherein they reside. No state shall make or enforce any law which shall abridge the privileges or immunities of citizens of the United States; nor shall any state deprive any person of life, liberty, or property, without due process of law; nor deny to any person within its jurisdiction the equal protection of the laws.

Section 2. Representatives shall be apportioned among the several states according to their respective numbers, counting the whole number of persons in each state, excluding Indians not taxed. But when the right to vote at any election for the choice of electors for President and Vice President of the United States, Representatives in Congress, the executive and judicial officers of a state, or the members of the legislature thereof, is denied to any of the male inhabitants of such state, being twenty-one years of age, and citizens of the United States, or in any way abridged, except for participation in rebellion, or other crime, the basis of representation therein shall be reduced in the proportion which the number of such male citizens shall bear to the whole number of male citizens twenty-one years of age in such state.

Section 3. No person shall be a Senator or Representative in Congress, or elector of President and Vice President, or hold any office, civil or military, under the United States, or under any state, who, having previously taken an oath, as a member of Congress, or as an officer of the United States, or as a member of any state legislature, or as an executive or judicial officer of any state, to support the Constitution of the United States, shall have engaged in insurrection or rebellion against the same, or given aid or comfort to the

enemies thereof. But Congress may by a vote of two-thirds of each house, remove such disability.

Section 4. The validity of the public debt of the United States, authorized by law, including debts incurred for payment of pensions and bounties for services in suppressing insurrection or rebellion, shall not be questioned. But neither the United States nor any state shall assume or pay any debt or obligation incurred in aid of insurrection or rebellion against the United States, or any claim for the loss or emancipation of any slave; but all such debts, obligations and claims shall be held illegal and void.

Section 5. The Congress shall have power to enforce, by appropriate legislation, the provisions of this article.

Article XV

Section 1. The right of citizens of the United States to vote shall not be denied or abridged by the United States or by any state on account of race, color, or previous condition of servitude.

Section 2. The Congress shall have power to enforce this article by appropriate legislation.

Article XVI

The Congress shall have power to lay and collect taxes on incomes, from whatever source derived, without apportionment among the several states, and without regard to any census or enumeration.

Article XVII

Section 1. The Senate of the United States shall be composed of two Senators from each state, elected by the people thereof, for six years; and each Senator shall have one vote. The electors in each state shall have the qualifications requisite for electors of the most numerous branch of the state legislature.

Section 2. When vacancies happen in the representation of any state in the Senate, the executive authority of such state shall issue writs of election to fill such vacancies: *Provided*, That the legislature of any state may empower the executive thereof to make temporary appointments until the people fill the vacancies by election as the legislature may direct.

Section 3. This amendment shall not be so construed as to affect the election or term of any Senator chosen before it becomes valid as part of the Constitution.

Article XVIII

Section 1. After one year from the ratification of this article the manufacture, sale, or transportation of intoxicating liquors within, the importation thereof into, or the exportation thereof from the United States and all territory subject to the jurisdiction thereof for beverage purposes is hereby prohibited.

Section 2. The Congress and the several states shall have concurrent power to enforce this article by appropriate legislation.

Section 3. This article shall be inoperative unless it shall have been ratified as an amendment to the Constitution by the legislatures of the several states, as provided in the Constitution, within seven years from the date of the submission hereof to the states by the Congress.

Article XIX

Section 1. The right of citizens of the United States to vote shall not be denied or abridged by the United States or by any state on account of sex.

Section 2. Congress shall have power to enforce this article by appropriate legislation.

Article XX

Section 1. The terms of the President and Vice President shall end at noon on the 20th day of January, and the terms of Senators and Representatives at noon on the 3d day of January, of the years in which such terms would have ended if this article had not been ratified; and the terms of their successors shall then begin.

Section 2. The Congress shall assemble at least once in every year, and such meeting shall begin at noon on the 3d day of January, unless they shall by law appoint a different day.

Section 3. If, at the time fixed for the beginning of the term of the President, the President elect shall have died, the Vice President elect shall become President. If a President shall not have

been chosen before the time fixed for the beginning of his term, or if the President elect shall have failed to qualify, then the Vice President elect shall act as President until a President shall have qualified; and the Congress may by law provide for the case wherein neither a President elect nor a Vice President elect shall have qualified, declaring who shall then act as President, or the manner in which one who is to act shall be selected, and such person shall act accordingly until a President or Vice President shall have qualified.

Section 4. The Congress may by law provide for the case of the death of any of the persons from whom the House of Representatives may choose a President whenever the right of choice shall have devolved upon them, and for the case of the death of any of the persons from whom the Senate may choose a Vice President whenever the right of choice shall have devolved upon them.

Section 5. Sections 1 and 2 shall take effect on the 15th day of October following the ratification of this article.

Section 6. This article shall be inoperative unless it shall have been ratified as an amendment to the Constitution by the legislatures of three-fourths of the several states within seven years from the date of its submission.

Article XXI

Section 1. The eighteenth article of amendment to the Constitution of the United States is hereby repealed.

Section 2. The transportation or importation into any state, territory, or possession of the United States for delivery or use therein of intoxicating liquors, in violation of the laws thereof, is hereby prohibited.

Section 3. This article shall be inoperative unless it shall have been ratified as an amendment to the Constitution by conventions in the several states, as provided in the Constitution, within seven years from the date of the submission hereof to the states by the Congress.

Article XXII

Section 1. No person shall be elected to the office of the President more than twice, and no person who has held the office of President, or acted as President, for more than two years of a term to which some other person was elected President shall be elected to the office of the President more than once. But this Article shall not apply to any person holding the office of President when this Article was proposed by the Congress, and shall not prevent any person who may be holding the office of President, or acting as President, during the term within which this Article becomes operative from holding the office of President or acting as President during the remainder of such term.

Section 2. This Article shall be inoperative unless it shall have been ratified as an amendment to the Constitution by the legislatures of three-fourths of the several states within seven years from the date of its submission to the states by the Congress.

Article XXIII

Section 1. The District constituting the seat of government of the United States shall appoint in such manner as the Congress may direct:

A number of electors of President and Vice President equal to the whole number of Senators and Representatives in Congress to which the District would be entitled if it were a state, but in no event more than the least populous state; they shall be in addition to those appointed by the states, but they shall be considered, for the purposes of the election of President and Vice President, to be electors appointed by a state; and they shall meet in the District and perform such duties as provided by the twelfth article of amendment.

Section 2. The Congress shall have power to enforce this article by appropriate legislation.

Article XXIV

Section 1. The right of citizens of the United States to vote in any primary or other election for President or Vice President, for electors for President or Vice President, or for Senator or Representative in Congress, shall not be denied or abridged by the United States or any State by reason of failure to pay any poll tax or other tax.

Section 2. The Congress shall have power to enforce this article by appropriate legislation.

Article XXV

Section 1. In case of the removal of the President from office or of his death or resignation, the Vice President shall become President.

Section 2. Whenever there is a vacancy in the office of the Vice President, the President shall nominate a Vice President who shall take office upon confirmation by a majority vote of both Houses of Congress.

Section 3. Whenever the President transmits to the President pro tempore of the Senate and the Speaker of the House of Representatives his written declaration that he is unable to discharge the powers and duties of his office, and until he transmits to them a written declaration to the contrary, such powers and duties shall be discharged by the Vice President as Acting President.

Section 4. Whenever the Vice President and a majority of either the principal officers of the executive departments or of such other body as Congress may by law provide, transmit to the President pro tempore of the Senate and the Speaker of the House of Representatives their written declaration that the President is unable to discharge the powers and duties of his office, the Vice President shall immediately assume the powers and duties of the office as Acting President.

Thereafter, when the President transmits to the President pro tempore of the Senate and the Speaker of the House of Representatives his written declaration that no inability exists, he shall resume the powers and duties of his office unless the Vice President and a majority of either the principal officers of the executive department or of such other body as Congress may by law provide, transmit within four days to the President pro tempore of the Senate and the Speaker of the House of Representatives their written declaration that the President is unable to discharge the powers and duties of his office. Thereupon Congress shall decide the issue, assemblying within forty-eight hours for that purpose if not in session. If the Congress, within twenty-one days after receipt of the latter written declaration, or, if Congress is not in session, within twenty-one days after Congress is required to assemble, determines by two-thirds vote of both Houses that the President is unable to discharge the powers and duties of his office, the Vice President shall continue to discharge the same as Acting President; otherwise, the President shall resume the powers and duties of his office.

Article XXVI

Section 1. The right of citizens of the United States, who are eighteen years of age or older, to vote shall not be denied or abridged by the United States or by any State on account of age.

Section 2. The Congress shall have power to enforce this article by appropriate legislation.

Appendix 8
Passport Application

DEPARTMENT OF STATE
PASSPORT APPLICATION
SEE INSTRUCTIONS—TYPE/PRINT IN INK IN WHITE AREAS

IDENTIFYING INFORMATION

NAME

FIRST/MIDDLE

LAST

MAILING ADDRESS (In Care Of if applicable, Street, City, State, ZIP Code)

☐ 5 yr. ☐ 10 yr.

R   D   O   DP   Endorsement

SEX	PLACE OF BIRTH	DATE OF BIRTH	SOCIAL SECURITY NUMBER

Male Female   City, State or Province, Country   Month Day Year   (Not Mandatory)

HEIGHT   COLOR OF HAIR   COLOR OF EYES   (Area Code) HOME PHONE   (Area Code) BUSINESS PHONE

Feet Inches   PERMANENT ADDRESS (Street, City, State, ZIP Code)   OCCUPATION   DEPARTURE DATE

FATHER'S FULL NAME   FATHER'S BIRTHPLACE AND FATHER'S BIRTH DATE (Mo., Day, Yr.)   FATHER U.S. CITIZEN?
Yes   No

MOTHER'S FULL MAIDEN NAME   MOTHER'S BIRTHPLACE AND MOTHER'S BIRTH DATE (Mo., Day, Yr.)   MOTHER U.S. CITIZEN?
Yes   No

PREVIOUS PASSPORT INFORMATION
HAVE YOU EVER BEEN ISSUED OR INCLUDED IN A U.S. PASSPORT?   Yes   No   IF YES, COMPLETE NEXT LINE REGARDING MOST RECENT PASSPORT. SUBMIT PASSPORT IF AVAILABLE

NAME IN WHICH ISSUED   PASSPORT NUMBER   ISSUE DATE   DISPOSITION OF PASSPORT
Month Day Year   (Submitted, Lost, etc.)

PROPOSED TRAVEL PLANS AND EMERGENCY ADDRESS (Not Mandatory)
LENGTH OF STAY   COUNTRIES TO BE VISITED

PERSON TO NOTIFY IN CASE OF EMERGENCY ABROAD (Not Traveling With You)
NAME IN FULL

ADDRESS

(Street, City, State, ZIP Code)

PHONE NUMBER   RELATIONSHIP
(Area Code)

MARRIAGE INFORMATION
HAVE YOU EVER BEEN MARRIED?   IF YES: DATE OF MOST RECENT MARRIAGE
Yes   No   Month Day Year

WIFE'S FULL MAIDEN NAME/HUSBAND'S FULL LEGAL NAME   SPOUSE'S PLACE OF BIRTH   SPOUSE'S DATE OF BIRTH   U.S. CITIZEN?
City, State or Province, Country   Month Day Year   Yes   No

IF WIDOWED/DIVORCED, CHECK BELOW AND GIVE DATE
WIDOWED   DIVORCED   Month Day Year

DO NOT SIGN APPLICATION UNTIL REQUESTED TO DO SO BY ACCEPTANCE AGENT
I have not, since acquiring United States citizenship, performed any of the acts listed under "Acts or Conditions" on the reverse of this application form (unless explanatory statement is attached). I solemnly swear (or affirm) that the statements made on this application are true and the photograph attached is a true likeness of me.

Subscribed and sworn to (affirmed) before me this

_____ Day of _____ 19 _____   (SEAL)   X

(To be signed by applicant in presence of acceptance agent)

Clerk of the _____   Postal Employee/
Passport Agent at _____

(Signature of person authorized to accept application)

FOR PASSPORT SERVICES USE ONLY   ☐ Birth Cert.   SR   CR   City   ☐ Passport   ☐ Naturalization/Citizenship Cert.

No.:   Filed/Issued;   Place: Bearer's Name:

☐ Other:
☐ Seen & Returned   Examiner Name
☐ Attached   Office, Date   FEE _____   EXEC. _____   POST _____

FORM DSP-11
(1-83)   (SEE INFORMATION ON REVERSE)   FORM APPROVED
OMB NO. 47-RO051

Photo area: 2" X 2", FROM 1" TO 1-3/8"

DEPARTMENT OF STATE
PASSPORT APPLICATION

HOW TO APPLY FOR A U.S. PASSPORT. U.S. passports are issued only to U.S. citizens or nationals. Each person must obtain his or her own passport.

IF YOU ARE A FIRST-TIME APPLICANT, please complete and submit this application personally with: (1) PROOF OF U.S. CITIZENSHIP; (2) PROOF OF IDENTITY; (3) TWO PHOTOGRAPHS; (4) FEES (as explained below) to one of the following acceptance agents: a clerk of any Federal or State court of record or a judge or clerk of any probate court, accepting applications; a designated postal employee at a selected post office; or an agent at a Passport Agency in Boston, Chicago, Honolulu, Houston, Los Angeles, Miami, New Orleans, New York, Philadelphia, San Francisco, Seattle, Stamford, or Washington, D.C.

IF YOU HAVE HAD A PREVIOUS PASSPORT, inquire about eligibility to use Form DSP-82 (mail-in application).

Address requests for passport amendment, extension of validity, or additional visa pages to a Passport Agency or a U.S. consulate or Embassy abroad. Check visa requirements with consular officials of countries to be visited.

(1) PROOF OF U.S. CITIZENSHIP

(a) APPLICANTS BORN IN THE UNITED STATES. Submit: previous U.S. passport; or, birth certificate. A birth certificate must include your given name and surname, date and place of birth, date the birth record was filed, and seal or other certification of the official custodian of such records. A record filed more than 1 year after birth is acceptable if it was supported by evidence described in the next paragraph.

IF NO BIRTH RECORD EXISTS, submit registrar's notice to that effect. Also submit an early baptismal or circumcision certificate, hospital birth record, early census, school, or family bible records, newspaper or insurance files, or notarized affidavits of persons having knowledge of your birth (preferably with at least one record listed above). Evidence should include your given name and surname, date and place of birth, and seal or other certification of office (if customary) and signature of issuing official.

(b) APPLICANTS BORN OUTSIDE OF THE UNITED STATES. Submit: previous U.S. passport; or Certificate of Naturalization; or Certificate of Citizenship; or evidence described below:

IF YOU CLAIM CITIZENSHIP THROUGH NATURALIZATION OF PARENT(S), submit your parent(s) Certificate(s) of Naturalization, your foreign birth certificate, and proof of your admission to the United States for permanent residence.

IF YOU CLAIM CITIZENSHIP THROUGH BIRTH ABROAD TO U.S. CITIZEN PARENT(S), submit a Consular Report of Birth (Form FS-240) or Certification of Birth (Form DS-1350 'or FS-545) or your foreign birth certificate, parents' marriage certificate, proof of parent(s) citizenship and affidavit of U.S. citizen parent(s) showing all periods and places of residence/physical presence in the United States and abroad before your birth.

(2) PROOF OF IDENTITY. If you are not personally known to the acceptance agent, submit one of the following items containing your signature AND physical description or photograph which is a good likeness of you: previous U.S. passport; Certificate of Naturalization or of Citizenship; driver's license (not temporary or learner's license); or Governmental (Federal, State, municipal) identification card or pass. Temporary or altered documents are not acceptable.

IF YOU CANNOT PROVE YOUR IDENTITY as stated above you must appear with an IDENTIFYING WITNESS, a U.S. citizen or permanent resident alien who has known you for at least 2 years. Your witness must prove his or her identity and complete and sign an "Affidavit of Identifying Witness" (Form DSP-71) before the acceptance agent. You must also submit some identification of your own.

(3) TWO PHOTOGRAPHS. Submit two identical photographs of you alone, sufficiently recent to be a good likeness (normally taken within the last 6 months), 2 x 2 inches in size, with an image size from bottom of chin to top of head (including hair) of between 1 and 1 3/8 inches. Photographs must be clear, front view, full face, taken in normal street attire without a hat or dark glasses, and printed on thin paper with a plain light (white or off-white) background. They may be in black and white or color. They must be capable of withstanding a mounting temperature of 225 degrees Fahrenheit (107 degrees Celsius). Photographs retouched so that your appearance is changed are unacceptable. Snapshots, most vending machine prints, and magazine or full-length photographs are unacceptable.

(4) FEES. Consult acceptance agent regarding amount of fees. Pay the passport and execution fees in one of the following forms: bank draft or cashier's check; check (certified, personal, travelers); money order (United States Postal, international currency exchange, bank); currency. Make passport and execution fee payable to Passport Services (except if applying at a State court, pay execution fee as the State court requires). No fee is charged to applicants with U.S. Government or military authorization for No-Fee passports (except State courts may collect the execution fee). Pay special postage if applicable.

PRIVACY ACT STATEMENT

The information solicited on this form is authorized by, but not limited to, those statutes codified in Titles 8, 18, and 22, United States Code, and all predecessor statutes whether or not codified, and all regulations issued pursuant to Executive Order 11295 of August 5, 1966. The primary purpose for soliciting the information is to establish citizenship, identity, and entitlement to issuance of a United States Passport or related facility, and to properly administer and enforce the laws pertaining thereto.

The information is made available as a routine use on a need-to-know basis to personnel of the Department of State and other government agencies having statutory or other lawful authority to maintain such information in the performance of their official duties; pursuant to a subpoena or court order; and, as set forth in Part 171, Title 22, Code of Federal Regulations (See *Federal Register*, Volume 42, pages 49791 through 49795).

Failure to provide the information requested on this form may result in the denial of a United States Passport, related document, or service to the individual seeking such passport, document, or service.

ACTS OR CONDITIONS

(If any of the below-mentioned acts or conditions has been performed by or applies to the applicant, the portion which applies should be lined out, and a supplementary explanatory statement under oath (or affirmation) by the applicant should be attached and made a part of this application.)

I have not, since acquiring United States citizenship, been naturalized as a citizen of a foreign state; taken an oath or made an affirmation or other formal declaration of allegiance to a foreign state; entered or served in the armed forces of a foreign state; accepted or performed the duties of any office, post, or employment under the government of a foreign state or political subdivision thereof; made a formal renunciation of nationality either in the United States or before a diplomatic or consular officer of the United States in a foreign state; or been convicted by a court or court martial of competent jurisdiction of committing any act of treason against, or attempting by force to overthrow, or bearing arms against, the United States, or conspiring to overthrow, put down, or to destroy by force, the Government of the United States.

WARNING: False statements made knowingly and willfully in passport applications or in affidavits or other supporting documents submitted therewith are punishable by fine and/or imprisonment under the provisions of 18 USC 1001 and/or 18 USC 1542. Alteration or mutilation of a passport issued pursuant to this application is punishable by fine and/or imprisonment under the provisions of 18 USC 1543. The use of a passport in violation of the restrictions contained therein or of the passport regulations is punishable by fine and/or imprisonment under 18 USC 1544. All statements and documents submitted are subject to verification.

FOR ACCEPTANCE AGENT'S USE ONLY (Applicant's Identifying Documents)

☐ PASSPORT ☐ CERTIFICATE OF NATURALIZATION OR CITIZENSHIP ☐ DRIVER'S LICENSE ☐ OTHER (Specify) _____ ISSUE DATE: Month ☐ Day ☐ Year ☐

EXPIRATION DATE: Month ☐ Day ☐ Year ☐ NUMBER _____ PLACE OF ISSUE _____ ISSUED IN THE NAME OF _____

FORM DSP-11
(1-83)

☆U.S. Government Printing Office: 1983—394-419

BUSINESS & FINANCE

HOW TO FORM YOUR OWN CALIFORNIA CORPORATION
All the forms, Bylaws, Articles, stock certificates and instructions necessary to file
your small profit corporation in California.
Calif. Edition $21.95

THE NON-PROFIT CORPORATION HANDBOOK: Includes all the forms, Bylaws, Articles &
instructions you need to form a non-profit
corporation in California.
Calif. Edition $21.95

BANKRUPTCY: DO IT YOURSELF: Step-by-step
instructions and all the forms you need.
National edition $14.95

LEGAL CARE FOR YOUR SOFTWARE: Protect your
software through the use of trade secret,
tradework, copyright, patent and contractual
laws and agreements. National Ed. $24.95

THE PARTNERSHIP BOOK: A basic primer for
people who are starting a small business
together. Sample agreements, buy-out
clauses, limited partnerships. $17.95

PLAN YOUR ESTATE: WILLS, PROBATE AVOIDANCE,
TRUSTS & TAXES: Making a will, alternatives
to probate, limiting inheritance & estate
taxes, living trusts, etc. $15.95

CHAPTER 13: THE FEDERAL PLAN TO REPAY YOUR
DEBTS: The alternative to straight bankruptcy. This book helps you develop a plan
to pay your debts over a 3 year period.
All forms & worksheets included. $12.95

BILLPAYERS' RIGHTS: Bankruptcy, student
loans, bill collectors & collection agencies, credit cards, car repossessions,
child support, etc. $10.95

THE CALIFORNIA PROFESSIONAL CORPORATION
HANDBOOK: All the forms & instructions
to form a professional corporation. $21.95

SMALL TIME OPERATOR: How to start &
operate your own small business, keep
books, pay taxes. $8.95

WE OWN IT!: Legal, tax & management
information you need to operate co-ops
& collectives. $9.00

FAMILY & FRIENDS

HOW TO DO YOUR OWN DIVORCE: All the
forms for an uncontested dissolution.
Calif. Edition $12.95

CALIFORNIA MARRIAGE & DIVORCE LAW:
Community & separate property, debts,
children, buying a house, etc. Sample
marriage contracts, simple will, probate avoidance information. $14.95

AFTER THE DIVORCE: HOW TO MODIFY
ALIMONY, CHILD SUPPORT & CHILD CUSTODY:
How to increase alimony or child support, decrease what you pay, change custody & visitation, etc. $14.95

THE LIVING TOGETHER KIT: Legal guide
for unmarried couples. Sample will &
living together contract. $14.95

SOURCEBOOK FOR OLDER AMERICANS: Most
comprehensive resource tool on income,
rights & benefits of Americans over 55.
Social security, Medicare, etc. $10.95

HOW TO ADOPT YOUR STEPCHILD: How to
prepare all forms & appear in court.
                                $14.95

A LEGAL GUIDE FOR LESBIAN/GAY COUPLES:
Raising children, buying property, wills,
etc. $14.95

RULES & TOOLS

THE PEOPLE'S LAW REVIEW: A compendium of
people's law resources. 50-state catalog
of self-help law materials; articles &
interviews. $8.95

FIGHT YOUR TICKET: Radar, drunk driving,
preparing for court, arguing your case,
cross-examining witnesses, etc. $12.95

LEGAL RESEARCH: HOW TO FIND AND UNDERSTAND
THE LAW: Comprehensive guide to doing
your own legal research. $12.95

CALIFORNIA TENANTS' HANDBOOK: Everything
tenants need to know to protect themselves. $9.95

EVERYBODY'S GUIDE TO SMALL CLAIMS COURT:
Step-by-step guide to going to small
claims court. $9.95

HOW TO CHANGE YOUR NAME: All the forms &
instructions you need. $14.95

PROTECT YOUR HOME WITH A DECLARATION OF
HOMESTEAD: All the forms & instructions
to homestead your home. $8.95

MARIJUANA: YOUR LEGAL RIGHTS: All the
legal information users & growers need to
guarantee their constitutional rights &
protect their privacy. $9.95

AUTHOR LAW: Comprehensive explanation of
the legal rights of authors. $14.95

UNEMPLOYMENT BENEFITS HANDBOOK: Everything you need to know about your benefits. $5.95

LANDLORDING: Maintenance and repairs,
getting good tenants, avoid evictions,
taxes, etc. $15.00

YOUR FAMILY RECORDS: How to Preserve
Personal, Financial and Legal History
Probate avoidance, joint ownership of
property, genealogical research. $12.95

MEDIA LAW A Legal Handbook for the
Working Journalist For anyone who
desires a better understanding of how
the law and journalism intersect. $14.9

in a lighter vein....

MURDER ON THE AIR An unconventional
murder mystery set in Berkeley, Calif.
                                   $5.95

29 REASONS NOT TO GO TO LAW SCHOOL: A
humorous and irreverent look at the
dubious pleasures of going to law school
                                   $6.9

Order Form

QUANTITY	TITLE	UNIT PRICE	TOTAL

Prices subject to change

☐ Please send me a
   catalogue of your books

Tax: (California only) 6½% for Bart,
     Los Angeles, San Mateo & Santa
     Clara counties; 6% for all others

Name_____

Address_____

_____

☐ I am not on Nolo's mailing list and would like to be.
  (If you receive the NOLO NEWS you are on the list and
  need not check the box.)

SUBTOTAL _____

Tax _____

Postage & Handling $1.00

TOTAL _____

Send to:

NOLO PRESS
950 Parker St.
Berkeley, CA 94710
        or

NOLO DISTRIBUTING
Box 544
Occidental, CA 95465